A Western Horseman Book

REINING

Completely Revised

The Guide for Training & Showing
Winning Reining Horses

By Al Dunning

With Pat Close

Photographs by Kathy Kadash

REINING
COMPLETELY REVISED

Published by
Western Horseman Inc.

3850 North Nevada Ave.
Box 7980
Colorado Springs, CO 80933-7980

Design, Typography, and Production
Western Horseman
Colorado Springs, Colorado

Cover photograph by
Rick Swan

Printing
Publisher's Press
Salt Lake City, Utah

Second Printing: May 1999

ISBN 0-911647-39-2

DEDICATION

I have been blessed with a wonderful,
supportive family and many friends. My friends have enriched
my life and made me realize how much I appreciate my
occupation as a horse trainer. My family has taught me many
of life's greatest lessons: to be thankful for success yet
humble in victory, and grateful for our many blessings. They
are the foundation of my life.

I love and respect my family and friends,
and dedicate this book to them.

AL DUNNING

INTRODUCTION

TODAY'S REINING horse evolved from the cowboy's ranch horse, whose job is to gather, move, hold, and sort cattle on the open range. A cowboy needs an agile saddle horse who is quick on his feet, can be controlled by a light rein, and has an explosive start and stop.

In years gone by, cowboys and vaqueros prided themselves on riding these hard-working horses and enjoyed challenging one another to see whose mount could stop faster or slide farther, and turn around with more speed. It was the beginning of the reining horse competition we know today.

Reining developed on the West Coast, where it was first referred to as stock horse competition. For many years, exhibitors showed "stock horses," not "reining horses." Gradually this event spread eastward where it was known as reining and where its popularity soared. And it was in the East, in such states as Ohio, where the finesse in today's reining horse originated. In fact, Dale Wilkinson, who was living in Ohio at the time, is considered the "father" of modern reining.

As a spectator event, reining ranks as one of the most popular in the equine world. The excitement it generates is assurance that reining will have a strong

In 1995 at the Reno Spectacular I won the gelding reining stakes on Codys Kid Too, owned by Tom Chambers of North Ogden, Utah.

Photo by Gail Bates

role in future equine competition.

Reining's popularity has also spread worldwide to Europe, Japan, and Brazil. Such countries as Germany, England, Italy, and Austria, for example, have been strong markets for proven reining horses, as well as for prospects and breeding stock. There are now breeding farms in Europe producing good reining horse prospects who represent the most popular bloodlines.

Almost every major breed association offers reining classes, but the organization that gets the lion's share of credit for popularizing the event is the National Reining Horse Association. Through NRHA leadership, reining has become an industry that offers substantial financial rewards, not only in purse money, but also in breeding, raising, and training these athletic horses.

Yet it's relatively easy for a newcomer or beginner to break into NRHA reining horse competition because the association offers classes for every skill level.

The future of reining horses has never looked brighter. The NRHA is growing, with an ever-increasing number of members and affiliate organizations throughout the world. And thanks to non-pro reining events in NRHA, AQHA, and other breed associations, more amateurs are getting involved. In fact, the AQHA has now made it possible for individual shows, at their discretion, to split the amateur reining into two age groups: 49-and-under and 50-and-over.

Amateurs as well as pros in other riding disciplines are finding that reining offers a challenge. It's an incomparable thrill to be

Grand Star Lady sliding in my home arena. When this picture was taken, the mare was owned by Tom Chambers of North Ogden, Utah.

Photo by HoofPrints

astride a horse spinning so fast that everything blurs, or running down the arena at a high rate of speed, locking down, and sliding 20 or 30 feet.

Reining is a great sport with its roots straight from the American West. It has been extremely rewarding to my family and myself, and it is with pleasure that I share with you through this book some of my ideas on training the reining horse. I hope the book will be helpful to every reader, rider, and spectator.

—*Al Dunning*

CONTENTS

1 SELECTING THE HORSE

There are many bloodlines capable of producing good reining horses.

BREEDING IS the first thing I consider when I'm looking for a young reining prospect. Ideally, I want a prospect to be sired by a horse who has proven himself—a horse who has been a reining champion and who has shown that he can get on his hocks and use himself in a highly physical manner, or, more important, has proven he can sire great-minded athletes.

I would also like this prospect to be out of a mare who has either won or, more important, has produced foals who have won. Many mares who win in the show ring never produce any good performers.

If you buy a colt or filly out of a mare who has already produced a winning reining horse, you have a better chance of getting a good one, even if the foal is by a different sire than his half-brother or sister.

As far as particular bloodlines, there are many capable of producing good reining horses. I feel that as long as you stick with proven bloodlines, you'll probably do okay. Most of today's proven sires all have strong foundation breeding. They go back to such horses as King P-234, Leo, Hollywood Gold, Three Bars (TB), Doc Bar, Sugar Bars, and Doc O'Lena. The

Here is a well-balanced horse with athletic conformation, good withers, and the "reiner look."

8

list continues to grow with succeeding generations.

Breeders today feel they are very successful with what they are breeding, but they are constantly looking for a pure outcross—a bloodline totally unrelated to the popular bloodlines of today. We've had the same popular bloodlines for many years now, and we have crossed them in so many ways that a lot of the good horses are closely related. Breeding some of these individuals to each other is getting dangerously close to inbreeding. I've seen the results of inbreeding, and they are not good. The temperament, straightness of legs, hoof size, bone structure, and general soundness have not been adequate.

Sometimes you'll stumble onto a good reining horse who wasn't bred to be one, but just happened to be born with the right kind of conformation, ability, and desire. Since he's so unusual, there's no way you can look for that kind. He's what we call a freak of nature. It's better—and a lot easier—to start with the right breeding, then look for the right kind of conformation and attitude.

Generally speaking, you don't want a halter-type horse. You seldom see top halter horses competing in performance classes because they are often too heavily muscled to be athletic, or because they are not pretty movers. Look at defensive linemen and compare them to track and basketball players. Most linemen can't begin to run and turn around and jump like those other guys can. You can make the same analogy between today's top halter horses and performance horses.

The reining prospect must be structurally sound, because this gives him an automatic physical advantage. He should not have major faults such as crooked legs; straight hocks or sickle hocks; a short, thick neck; long back; weak loins; or too much width in his chest. He's got to look like he has the strength, agility, and other features it takes to make a great reining horse.

These are only generalities, however, because a horse with a great mind and a great heart can overcome some physically limiting factors. But you can't tell what kind of heart and mind he has until he's old enough to ride . . . and sometimes when you are buying, you only have a short time to look at a prospect.

General Guidelines

Over the years I have formulated some general guidelines that I always follow to maximize the chances of choosing a potential champion. One of them is size. I like an average-size horse, say 14.3 to 15.1 hands. A horse who's too small doesn't have the physical strength it takes to show in reining over a long period. By a small horse, I mean one who stands maybe 14.2 or shorter and has small bone. He will be more prone to break down.

Now I know a lot of people will say little horses can be tough, but they're probably talking about stamina for endurance. I'm using the term *small* as it relates to muscle and bone structure, and their ability to hold up under the physical stress to which a reining horse is subjected.

A horse who's too large usually doesn't have the quickness and agility that a reining horse should have. Again, this is a generality because there are some 16-hand horses who are pretty movers and who can stop and spin, but they are the exception. Horses with massive muscles, thick and heavy shoulders, deep bodies, and a wide front end do not adapt well to this event either.

The reining prospect should have adequate bone to stay sound, and a good-sized foot to avoid problems such as navicular disease. It doesn't hurt if he toes out a little in front, but if he's toed way out, he could have problems galloping pretty or turning around well. Also, when the bones in the front legs are not aligned correctly, the resulting stress can result in unsoundnesses.

When turning around (spinning), the front legs of the toed-out horse are prone to interfere with each other. This can result in injured coronet bands, splints, sesamoiditis, ruptured tendons, and other physical problems. Also, the horse can't turn smooth and flat when the outside foot is pointing in the wrong direction. As the horse is turning around, that leg can't flex properly to cross over the inside leg.

A horse who's too large usually doesn't have the quickness and agility that a reining horse should have.

This horse has a good front end with relatively straight legs, about the right amount of width to his chest, and a good V, which is actually an upside-down V. Another plus: He doesn't have heavy shoulders that would impede him in making turnarounds.

For example, suppose a toed-out horse is turning to the left. Because his right front leg points to the right, the horse will tend to keep that leg stiff and use his shoulder to push it around to the left, making it difficult for that leg to cross over the left. When the horse turns to the right, he has the same problem if his left leg toes out.

Toeing-in is not good either, for some of the same reasons just described. Both toeing-in and toeing-out radically decrease the stride length, and also go hand-in-hand with unsoundness problems.

To be a good stopper, a horse must be structurally correct in the hind legs. The hocks should be strong, durable, and well-made because of the great stress placed on them when the horse stops.

Looking at the hocks from the side, they should be correct; however, I don't mind if they have a little bend or set to them. I prefer that over hocks too straight. You also have to look at where the hocks are in relation to an imaginary plumb line dropped from the point of the buttocks. A true sickle-hocked horse is absolutely undesirable because unsoundness can result. Typically, that horse is not going to be much of a stopper either, and is predisposed to curb and stifle problems. However, when a horse's hocks are under him and have only a slight set to them, he's already in a semi-stopping position.

From the rear view, the hocks should be straight to provide the strength the horse needs for stopping, although I've had some pretty good stoppers who were slightly cow-hocked, or bow-legged. You would think that their legs couldn't hold a slide or that their legs would splay out or cross, but it's amazing what some horses can do.

I don't like horses who are extremely wide between the hocks. These horses will track wide and are seldom good movers. Horses who are narrow behind are usually better movers who can also stop straighter than can horses who are extreme wide-trackers. Horses should also be wider at the stifles than they are at the hocks.

From the hocks down, the legs should be straight, when looking at them from the rear.

The Hindquarters

If I were to draw the perfect reining horse, I'd draw one with powerful hindquarters. They are the basis of a reining horse because he's got to use his hind end, and to do so, he needs strength. But although I want a horse with muscle in the hindquarters, I don't want overmuscling, like the massive muscling in some halter horses. I want long, strong muscling through the hip and down into the stifle, especially the inside of the gaskin and stifle. I love a horse who is strong in the stifle. He can really get into the ground and stop, and he can hold his stop in any kind of ground.

A horse with a weak stifle may be able to slide along the surface, but he usually can't handle a stop in deeper ground. He is also more apt to injure himself in the stifle or hock joint.

My kind of horse should also have a long hip and strong loin. I like a reining horse to bend in the loin when he stops, so he can really get in the ground and push with his hindquarters. He's got to push his back feet forward in order to balance himself as his momentum shifts from his forehand to his hindquarters during stops. He can't do this with a weak loin.

His back should be medium in length—not too short because it needs some length for flexibility to arc or bend properly, and not too long or it will lack strength.

The horse definitely should have good withers to keep the saddle in the middle of the back. Very few great stopping horses have mutton withers. Typically, a mutton-withered horse lacks flexibility and length in his stride.

The best horses have a big hip, powerful stifle, medium back, and good withers. They all tie together. Plus good withers usually go along with a good neck. Look at mutton-withered horses and you'll find very few with well-shaped, flexible-type necks.

I like a medium-length neck with a top line that flows into the poll, so the poll has some curve to it instead of being flat and stiff. That kind of poll isn't supple and therefore cannot flex easily.

The bottom line of the neck should be shorter than the top line, and also be straight. The opposite—an upright neck with a longer bottom line—is called a ewe neck (because sheep have this type neck). This "upside-down" type of neck

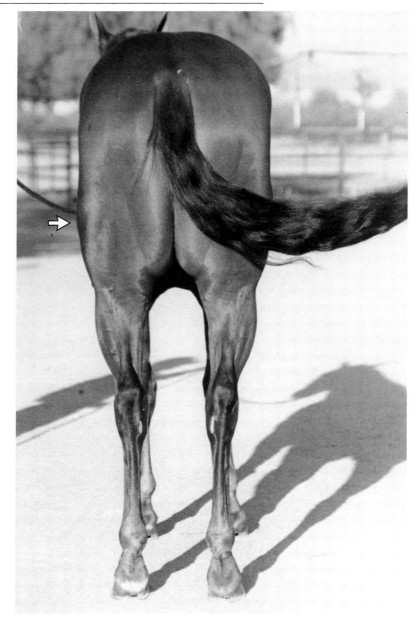

A relatively good set of hind legs. However, I would like to see the stifles with a little more muscling (arrow).

11

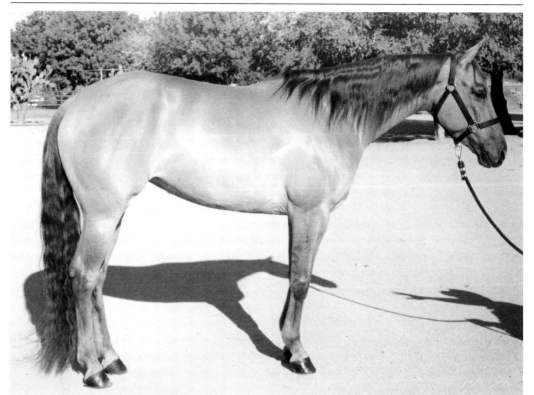

This mare has a good top line, withers, and neck, and a clean throatlatch. Note how the top line of the neck flows into the poll and is longer than the bottom line. On the negative side, this mare is lightly muscled and slightly over at the knee. Nonetheless, she was a finalist in the 1995 NRHA Non-Pro Futurity.

Although I don't believe there is any correlation between a pretty head and intelligence, Boomernic certainly has both a handsome head and lots of smarts. He also has exceptional athletic ability, and won the 1992 NRHA Futurity with one of my former students, Brett Stone, as his trainer-rider.

Photo by Cappy Jackson

will not flex properly.

You don't want an excessively long neck on a reining horse because you will lose some control. When I touch a horse on the neck with the rein, I want his head, poll, and crest—his entire neck—to turn. If the neck is excessively long, it might not be as controllable as I want it to be.

I don't want a short neck or a thick neck because they lack flexibility; they don't bend laterally or vertically like they should. The best kind of neck is refined and of medium length.

Although the shoulder should be balanced and sloping, to me, the most important feature about the shoulder is its size. A horse with massive, heavily muscled shoulders, with the legs out on the points, lacks agility and handiness. So does a horse with a wide chest. He generally can't cross over with his front legs when he turns around, and won't have the "athletic reach" it takes to stretch out in the rundown, and then use his front legs properly in the stop.

But I don't want the horse pinched (too narrow) in the chest either. He needs a pretty good V (which is actually an upside-down V), so he has enough width for

Until you ride a horse long enough to determine his athletic ability, heart, and mind, you can only judge him on his breeding, conformation, and way of going. This horse has proven that she has what it takes to be a good reiner.

A horse with thick lips or a fat muzzle usually isn't as sensitive and won't respond to the bit as well as a horse with thinner lips.

strength and to move well, but not so much width that he moves like a truck.

It doesn't make much difference how pretty the head is on a reining horse. But personally, I like to ride a good-looking horse, and sometimes good looks can add to your score. If a judge has two horses who work about equally, but one's prettier than the other, the better-looker will probably win. However, "pretty is as pretty does."

Contrary to what some people think, I don't believe there's any correlation between a pretty head and intelligence. There are horses with beautiful heads who aren't very smart.

Some trainers, including me, like horses with what we refer to as workmanlike heads. These horses have intelligent, "can-do" expressions even though their heads might not necessarily be perfect.

I do believe that the length of the mouth affects how good a horse might be as a reiner. When a horse has a long (deep) mouth, often he's the kind who will open his mouth when you pull on the bridle. Usually he has a tall roof to his mouth, too, and won't be as sensitive in the bridle. And if he has a stout lower jaw, he might take ahold of the bit and pull on you.

A horse with a shallow mouth usually has the capability to carry a bit better, and also be more responsive to the bit because he will generally have a lower roof to his mouth. This is good when you are using a bit with a higher port, such as a half-breed, that works off the roof of the mouth, as well as the bars and chin groove. Then when you simply pick up the reins, that signals the horse that you're going to ask him to do something because he feels the port move in his mouth. That allows you to take a lighter hold of his chin (with the curb chain). When a horse is alerted that you're going to ask him for a maneuver, he's ready and responds more accurately.

The thickness of the lips is another factor to keep in mind. A horse with thick lips or a fat muzzle usually isn't as sensitive and won't respond to the bit as well as a horse with thinner lips. It's just like a horse with thin skin; you don't have to cue him as firmly as you do one with a thick hide.

As for color, a good horse is a good horse, regardless of color. Some of the

13

I'm holding a quality 2-year-old prospect with a balanced look about her, an intelligent head, medium-length neck, nice hip, and long, athletic muscling.

greatest reining horses today are bays, chestnuts, sorrels, palominos, and buckskins. This is because there are more horses of those colors, and because some of the great sires and dams of today are of those colors, and are passing their color to their offspring.

It doesn't bother me what color a horse is as long as his heart and mind are good, and those factors are the hardest to determine. We can't judge them until we ride the horse, although we can get a general idea by working with a horse on the ground. If he's bull-headed or ill-tempered during halter-breaking and other early handling, he'll probably be that way under saddle.

When it's possible, I like to turn a young horse loose in a pen and watch him move.

It's better to get him by himself to evaluate him, such as in a round corral. Usually the better horses have a spark to them, with a good look in their eyes. They are inquisitive, but a little leary of what's going on. They will stand quietly, but when you move at them, they jump away quickly, then stop and turn around to see what you're doing. Those who just stand there and look at you, or turn tail and keep on running, are seldom as trainable.

My Ideal Reining Horse

It was in the 1960s when I first started showing reining horses, or stock horses as they were known then in the Southwest and on the West Coast. Although I have had some great horses in my career, my all-time favorite is still Expensive Hobby, whom I showed in the 1970s and early 1980s. Even today, if I were to profile my ideal reining horse, it would have to be Expensive Hobby.

When this buckskin gelding was 3 years old (in 1973), I bought him for Georganna Stewart of Yuma, Ariz., because he fit the mold I like. Since he turned out to be one

14

Even though he was retired in 1983, Expensive Hobby is still my ideal reining horse, as well as my all-time favorite.

Photo by Don Trout

of the greatest reining horses in the country, he proved those ideals to be correct.

When he was running a pattern, he was a big, stout, powerful, well-oiled piece of machinery. But when people saw him unsaddled, standing quietly or relaxed in his stall, they were surprised because he didn't look like the same horse they saw in the arena. He was personable and quiet in the stall, and not as big as he seemed to be in the show arena where his ring presence was so dynamic.

When I stood back and analyzed him, he had everything I liked. He was the right size, standing 15 hands. He was not too wide in front; he had a shallow mouth and nice big eyes; his ears set well; he had a nice neck and a good set of withers; and his back was just the right length. He was

strong through the loins; and had a big, long hip and good tailset. He was powerful in the hindquarters, and stout in the stifle. He had fancy hocks that were big, strong, close to the ground, and set under him just right. And he had a flexible, physical look about him.

To add icing to the cake, he had the right kind of mind and heart. He was solid, dependable, and honest . . . and he was one in a million.

15

2 EQUIPMENT

If the horse is irritated by an ill-fitting saddle, he can't be expected to perform to the best of his ability.

This is the typical outfit I use when schooling: a headstall and snaffle bit, running martingale, and breast collar. I use the latter when necessary to help stabilize the saddle.

I AM VERY particular about the type of equipment I use because it can make a definite difference in my safety, the horse's comfort, and how we perform together. If, for example, the saddle doesn't fit me properly, I can't ride to the best of my ability, and therefore I will inhibit what the horse is trying to do. Or if the horse is irritated by an ill-fitting saddle or something else pinching or rubbing him, he can't be expected to perform to the best of his ability.

Bridles

I prefer all of my snaffle-bit headstalls to be made of good-quality leather with both a browband and throatlatch. I don't like most one-ear headstalls for snaffles for two reasons: 1/ They sometimes allow the bit to lie crooked (one side higher than the other) in the horse's mouth. 2/ Sometimes when you're riding with a snaffle and pull the reins, the action of the bit

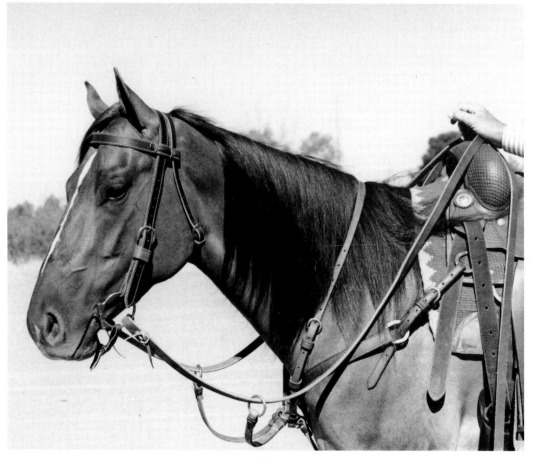

16

causes the bridle to press on the ear at the same time, or even slip off the head or down the neck. A horse can also shake or rub off a one-ear bridle pretty easily.

A headstall with a browband and throatlatch is also more secure when bitting up a young horse, or tying his head around.

I do ride most of my bridle horses in a split-ear headstall, but the earpiece is made properly and is of sufficient size so it fits correctly, allowing the bit to hang straight.

I like good leather for stoutness and safety. With proper care, headstalls and other leather gear should also last a long time.

Every time I put a bridle on a horse, I check it for safety. Although I don't like Chicago screws because they tend to work loose, most of my headstalls have them, and I always make sure they are tight.

I like to use a leather chin strap on a snaffle to keep the bit from sliding through the mouth; the strap applies no pressure. I fasten it below the reins on the rings. On most horses I ride with a curb bit, I use a flat curb chain. But horses who are real light and sensitive in the mouth may only need a leather chin strap; this preserves the sensitivity of the chin groove.

Reins

On my snaffle bridles, I ride with reins ⅞-inch wide that are made of good harness leather. New reins made of this leather are a little firm and might feel stiff until they are broke in, but they limber up into good-feeling reins with a lot of body. You can use them for several years. New reins that are already limber will later become too limp and feel like a dish rag. This will not allow me the sensitivity that I try to develop in my horses.

Because I have large hands, I like a wider, heavier, snaffle-bit rein with a lot of body. Someone with smaller hands, however, would probably feel more comfortable with a lighter, ⅝-inch rein.

I don't like to oil my reins because that makes them too limber. Instead, I use a good-quality lanolin-based saddle soap. I secure almost all of my reins with leather ties, not snaps or buckles because they are liable to work loose. However, some romal reins are made with snaps for convenience.

A typical headstall used for showing in reining events.

Bits

Like most trainers, I have acquired a large number of bits, both snaffles and curbs. When I was showing in Arizona and California in the 1960s and '70s, I usually rode finished horses in ornate silver bits, many of which were halfbreeds. That was the style of the day on the West Coast. Bridle horses were shown on light rein contact and with their heads in a flexed position. Those heavier silver bits helped achieve the look we wanted. But now times have changed and trainers and exhibitors primarily show with plainer, lighter bits.

The bit I use depends on the individual horse's mouth, his level of training, and his particular needs. Is he light in the mouth? Or does he tend to get a little heavy and therefore need a bit with more leverage and weight? I also have to find a bit that the horse is happy with. Bits are a lot like boots or shoes. You can walk okay

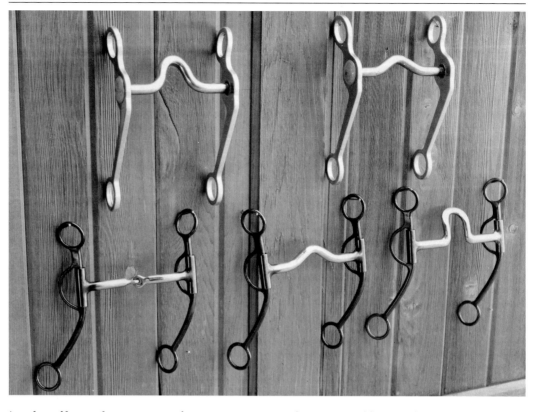

Here are five curb bits, made by Greg Darnall, that I use a lot on many different horses. On top are two grazer bits with aluminum shanks and iron mouthpieces. The one on the left has a medium port; the other a low port. On the bottom row left is a Loomis shanked snaffle, which is a great transition bit to be used after a regular snaffle bit, but before advancing to a curb bit with a ported mouthpiece. The other two bits also have Loomis shanks; the one in the middle has a low port; the one on the right, a spooned port.

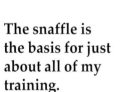

The snaffle is the basis for just about all of my training.

in a lot of boots, but some are far more comfortable than others. Bits feel the same way to a horse.

I use several types of mouthpieces in my bits, from a simple low port to a Salinas-type spoon. I seldom use rollers and copper covers anymore. I just don't feel they are necessary with the way we are showing and training our horses today.

The snaffle is the basis for just about all of my training. I like a smooth snaffle with a ³⁄₈-inch mouthpiece made of iron. Iron or cold steel works better in a horse's mouth than anything else, whereas aluminum and stainless steel do not work well. Iron will rust, and the rust has a more palatable taste in the mouth.

There is a time to use copper in the horse's mouth. Copper enhances the flow of saliva, which helps keep the mouth moist and therefore softer. In the old days, I always heard that a horse who slobbers is a horse with a good mouth, and I still believe that. Of course, a horse will also slobber excessively if he has an injured mouth.

Copper used by itself, however, is too soft, and a horse could chew through a snaffle made with straight copper. The best copper-mouthed snaffles have an iron core with copper over the top. In years past, I used twisted-wire copper snaffles made that way, but I don't any longer because they wore out so fast and developed sharp edges. The twisted-wire snaffles I use now are made of 100 percent iron.

My favorite snaffle was designed by Don Dodge and is made by Greg Darnall. I like it because it doesn't pinch the corners of the mouth, and because it has a little weight to it; when you loosen the reins, this snaffle drops in the mouth, quickly releasing the pressure. The horse can feel it better. With a real light bit, a horse can't easily tell when you have contact on the reins or when you turn them loose.

Once a horse is broke, he should feel you picking up the reins and start his reaction before you ever take hold of him. That is, if you are using the right bit with the right reins, and know how to use them. But I don't believe you can get this done with a lightweight bit and reins because the horse simply can't feel them. I have a variety of curb bits in my tack room. Most of them

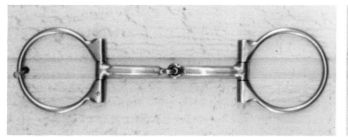

My favorite snaffle was designed by Don Dodge and is made by Greg Darnall.

A Don Dodge snaffle with a twisted-wire mouthpiece made of iron. This is a good schooling or training bit for a horse who needs to become lighter and more responsive.

are made by Greg Darnall and have 8-inch shanks and a variety of mouthpieces ranging from simple ports to higher-ported correctionals.

I also have a couple of spade bits that I now primarily use for bitting up horses. I loosen or remove the chin strap, take the slack out of the reins, and tie them to the saddle horn. I let the horse stand in his stall or move around the arena. When he sticks his nose out or leans on the bit, the mouthpiece raises up and presses against the roof of his mouth. He learns that when he brings his nose in and backs off the bit, the pressure is relieved. It teaches him not to lean on the bit. This is a good way to use a spade to develop sensitivity and a flexible poll for a better feel.

The use of the spade, because of its extra feel with the higher port, makes the horse give more readily because the roof of the mouth is so sensitive. If you bit up with a spade, however, be very careful because the pressure on the roof of the mouth might frighten a horse.

In fact, with a young horse, and especially one who has never been in a curb bit or bitted up, you should first bit him up with a snaffle or low-port curb before ever bitting him up with a spade.

A lower-port bit can also be effective for bitting up. When the horse leans on the bit, it affects the chin groove and the bars of the mouth, and a sensitive horse learns to yield to the pressure by dropping his head and bringing his nose in.

When I bit up a horse with a higher-port bit, I sometimes remove the curb chain for two reasons: 1/ I want him to learn to respond to a signal from the bit, not the curb chain. 2/ I'm trying to preserve the sensitivity in the chin groove as much as I can. I don't want to rough up that area and get it calloused because then it won't be as responsive to the curb chain or strap.

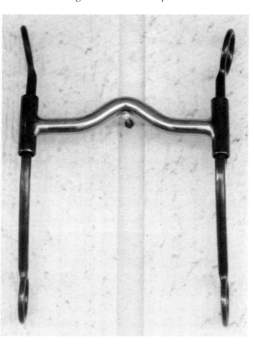

A low-port curb bit that offers minimal tongue relief. Note how the headstall rings are tipped out so they do not rub the horse.

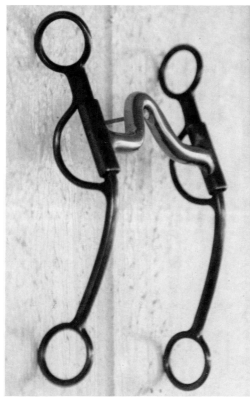

A medium-port bit that offers more tongue relief. The Loomis shanks are a standard 8 inches in length. The center rings can be used for attaching a set of snaffle reins. The curb strap should be attached to the top rings, not the center rings.

A grazer bit with a high port that I use on both cutting and reining horses. Because of its swept-back shanks, this bit gives a slower signal to the horse. This is good on an exceptionally responsive horse because a pull on the reins will not scare him.

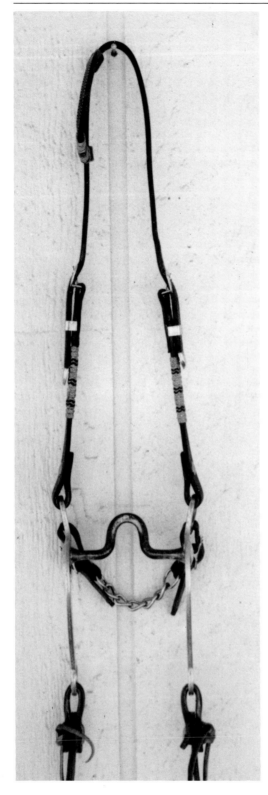

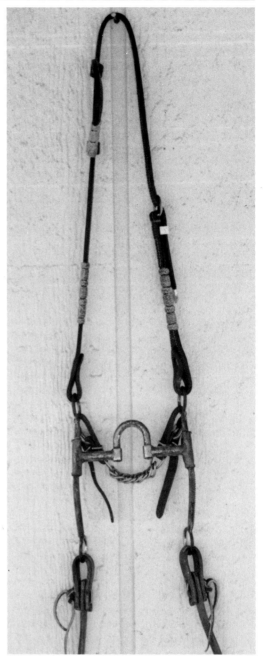

This is what's called a correction bit, although the term does not refer to any specific problem. Because of its pressure points, it is a bit used on more advanced horses.

Before you bridle a young horse, it's always good to check his mouth for any abnormalities. Have your veterinarian or equine dentist look for such problems as wolf teeth, loose teeth, injured tongue or bars, thistles or burs imbedded in the tongue or gums or caught between teeth, and sharp edges on teeth. Wolf teeth can interfere with the action of the bit, and sharp edges can cut the inside of the cheeks when the upper part of the bridle pushes against them. Have those teeth floated and any problem teeth pulled.

20

Here's a horse bitted up with a curb bit and romal reins. Note that the reins are adjusted so the horse gets relief when his face is vertical.

On a properly adjusted running martingale, the rings should come within an inch or two of the throatlatch when slack is taken out of the reins.

Running Martingale

The kind I like is made of leather, and it's a regular running martingale, not a rig you attach to the breast collar. The one I use snaps into a ring in the cinch and has a neck strap. It's also plenty long so it doesn't inhibit the horse until he gets his head out of position.

If a running martingale is adjusted too short, when you pull on the reins, you put pressure on the rings and therefore do not have direct contact with the mouth. This doesn't allow the horse to develop his natural head position, and the constant pressure from the bit will toughen the mouth. Eventually the horse could become less sensitive to pressure from the bit, meaning you will have to pull harder to get a response.

Draw reins and a nylon rope cavesson being used with a snaffle bit.

A draw rein snapped to the cinch ring.

On the other hand, if the martingale is too long, it doesn't do any good. I like to adjust mine so the rings come to the middle of the neck when you pull them straight up; or if you pull them toward the head, they should come within an inch or two of the throatlatch.

Cavessons

There are times when I want to use something on a horse to help him learn to keep his mouth closed. For this, I like a leather cavesson or a nylon-rope cavesson about a half-inch in diameter, with a barrel knot tied at the heel.

I adjust it so it hangs just below the bridge of the nose, and so I can fit two fingers underneath it. That allows him to open his mouth a little, so he doesn't feel trapped, but he can't open it wide.

When a horse is taught to keep his mouth closed, he is more responsive to the bit. Why? He has less leverage with his lower jaw to resist pressure from the bit.

However, I rarely use a cavesson on a green colt because I don't mind if he opens his mouth when I put pressure on the bit.

It's better for him to give his jaw by opening his mouth than to lock up and resist the pull of the reins.

If you trap a colt by tying his mouth shut, you can create resistance in his early stages of training. At first, he might drop his lower jaw and open his mouth, but as he learns to flex at the poll, he will keep his mouth closed when his head goes into a more vertical position.

If a rider has skillful hands, it won't be long until the colt will flex at the poll and keep his face vertical in response to a light pull.

Hackamores

My bosals vary from ¼-inch to ⅞-inch in diameter. All of them have a rawhide core with a rawhide or latigo cover. Since latigo is softer, I use those bosals on more sensitive horses. I like a long bosal (12-inch) with a good-size heel knot so the bosal drops away from the jaw when the pressure is released.

I also like some weight to my bosals. With a heavier bosal that rocks on the nose, the weight will assist in developing the proper head carriage.

Which bosal to use depends on the rider's preference and the individual horse, but keep in mind that a large bosal is not necessarily more severe. Sometimes a rawhide bosal that's small in diameter, but stiff, will really bite a horse. I don't want that because it will make a horse resistant.

I like a little bigger bosal, a ⅝- or ¾-inch, that has a little less "bite" so the horse won't resist it. In my opinion, a real big bosal, such as a ⅞-inch, is best for a big horse, or maybe one who's heavy-headed (not very responsive). Because he lacks sensitivity he needs to be bumped a little harder or have more weight on his head.

Sometimes I also use a big, loose bosal on a young horse. I want it to bounce around on his head because that encourages him to find a comfortable position in which to carry his head so the bosal doesn't bounce. Usually a comfortable position is the correct position.

I do not use a hackamore headstall complete with a fiador, etc., because I don't think it's necessary, especially in the show ring. Also, sometimes the fiador prevents the bosal from dropping away from the head when I release the pressure. I often use a leather string, tied to the cheeks of

I sometimes use a German martingale on a horse who is more resistant to positioning his head correctly. Whereas a running martingale is somewhat lenient in allowing a horse to stick his nose out or head up, a German martingale is not. It will allow the head to move up a little bit, but no farther.

With a willing, trainable horse, basic equipment such as a snaffle, running martingale, and cavesson are usually effective and all that's necessary.

the hackamore hanger (headstall) to keep the cheeks away from the horse's eyes.

If I think the cheeks of a bosal are too rough for a particular horse, I wrap them with electrical tape.

All of my hackamore reins (mecates) are made of mane hair, except for a few that have tail hairs mixed in. These mecates are approximately 22 feet long.

Miscellaneous Headgear

With a willing, trainable horse, basic equipment such as a snaffle, running martingale, and cavesson are usually effective and all that's necessary. But there are some horses who are tougher-minded and less trainable. On them we sometimes have to use other techniques and equipment that help us get the job done.

For example, on horses who are always leaning on the bridle and are heavy, or who don't want to relax their necks, we can use draw reins or a German martingale to assist us. On horses I'm having a difficult time slowing up or stopping in a snaffle or hackamore, I'll use something like a steel sidepull or an E-Z Stop on a temporary basis to get their attention.

Another problem: a horse who needs to stay in a snaffle so I can develop his lateral flexibility, but who keeps pulling on the bit. To lighten him up, I'll use a thinner wire snaffle.

Those are the standard pieces of equipment I use to help the typical horse understand what I am trying to teach him. But sometimes I'll have a talented horse who is somewhat difficult to train. I can't give up on him, so I often have to use alternative equipment. Then when I get the horse over the hump, I can go back to standard or traditional equipment.

Saddle Blankets

I use several kinds of saddle pads: fleece, orthopedic, and felt. The one I use on a horse depends on his conformation, and sometimes I have to try several pads to find the one that works best. For example, if he has heavy shoulders, withers too flat or too prominent, or a dry-spot problem, I'll use the particular pad that I think will be comfortable and functional to that horse. Dry spots are usually caused by pressure from a poor-fitting saddle; for example, a saddle whose bars are too narrow for a flat-withered horse. Eventually those dry spots usually develop white hairs. Sore backs and withers, sensitive loins, and spots with the hair rubbed off are other common signs of a poor-fitting saddle.

I don't like thick pads because the saddle will slip or roll unless you cinch extra tight, which I don't like to do. With the right tree in your saddle, so it fits your horse properly, you don't need a real thick pad. When I'm showing, I use a thin pad with a single Navajo over it for aesthetic value only.

Some riders use two pads, or one extra-thick pad, believing that it will compensate for a poor-fitting saddle. But that isn't always true. Too much padding might compound the problem, and force you to over-cinch your horse.

Some people overlook the importance of using a clean, proper-fitting saddle pad. A dirty, sweat-caked, hairy pad can irritate the horse, causing him to switch his tail and show other signs of irritation. It can also rub sores.

Saddles

The reining saddle I ride sits close to the horse's back and weighs about 40 pounds. The tree is the most important component in any saddle, and the tree in the saddle I ride has had lots of research behind it to make it fit properly on as many horses as possible. It also has quality leather and hardware and is made to last through many years of hard use.

A well-made saddle tends to stay more secure on the horse without having to cinch too tight. I only take one wrap with the latigo when I cinch the horse so

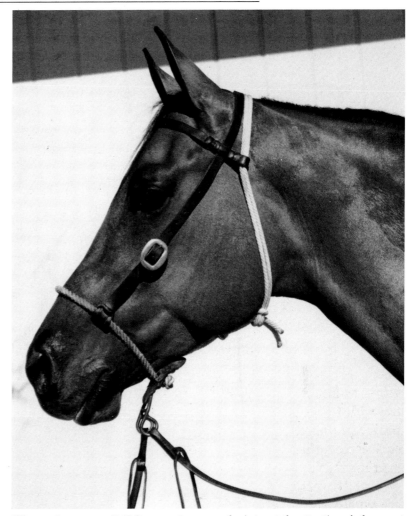

I'll sometimes use an E-Z Stop on a temporary basis to get the attention of a horse not responding properly to a snaffle or hackamore.

there is no bulk under my leg, which allows my leg to move freely and to better feel the horse. If you have to take two or more wraps, you probably need a shorter cinch.

A good saddle helps the rider stay in a balanced position. However, even with a proper-fitting saddle, a poor rider—who rides like a sack of potatoes and has poor horsemanship skills—can cause a horse's back to become sore.

The saddle should be positioned in the middle of the horse's back, not too far forward over the withers, or too far back over the loins. The gullet of the saddle should be of sufficient width so it does not pinch the side of the withers, but neither should

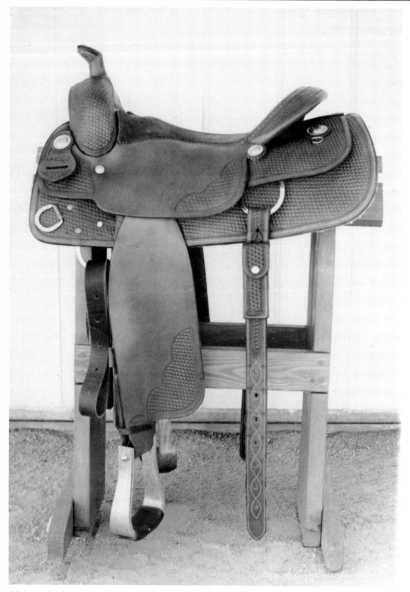

This is the basic reining saddle I use. This particular saddle has half-breed basket stamping. It's handcrafted by Bob's Custom Saddles in Scottsdale.

movement, holding him in one place. The seat I like is built up slightly in front, but is fairly flat where the rider sits, so he is positioned in the middle of the saddle. When the saddle is in the middle of the horse's back, and you are in the middle of the saddle, that is the proper riding position.

The length of the seat is determined by the size of the rider's seat and thighs. The rider should have a couple of inches of room between his back pockets and the cantle, and an equal amount of space in front. I see far more saddles that are too short in the seat for riders than the opposite. A rider simply can't ride properly in a seat too short because he's pinned against the cantle and cannot move properly in motion with the horse.

Women in particular often ride a saddle with a seat too short. They believe that because women are usually shorter in height and weigh less than men, they need a shorter seat. However, proper seat length is not only determined by size and weight, but also by size of hips, seat, and thighs.

I like moderate swells and a horn that's low. If it's high, then I have to raise my hand higher to rein the horse.

I have saddles whose riggings are in the tree, and saddles whose riggings are in the skirt. I like in-skirt rigging because there is no bulk under my legs, and the saddle is slightly lighter. Rigging on the tree is stouter, but not necessary unless you plan to rope.

Flat-bottom stirrups that are 2½ inches wide are the ones I use the most. This type of stirrup allows me to ride on the balls of my feet with my heels down, which is good horsemanship.

Proper length of the fenders should not be overlooked. Correct length is determined by the inseam of the rider's legs. If a fender is too short for a long-legged rider, it can pinch his leg at the top of his boot, as well as on his thigh or knee at the top of the fender. If a fender is too long for a short-legged rider, the fender will be jammed up into the tree, preventing it from swinging properly. This, in turn, prevents the rider from using his legs correctly, and can also

it press down on the top of the withers. This can cause discomfort or pain to the horse, affecting how he moves, causing him to become short-strided and ill-tempered as well.

I like a saddle with a low cantle and a comfortable seat that is not built up excessively; that type of seat restricts the rider's cause the rider to lose his stirrups.

A fender whose top doesn't fit under the seat jockey can also pinch a rider on the thigh.

Protective Boots

I always use protective boots on the front legs for two reasons: They protect the horse from hurting himself, and the right kind of boots provide leg support. Boots, of course, must be put on correctly so they provide the support and protection for which they are intended.

Bell boots are used on the front feet. They protect the bulb or heel when a horse overreaches with a back foot while stopping. Bell boots also protect the coronet band if the opposite foot strikes it when the horse is turning around. A horse cannot perform properly if he's hurt, or if he's afraid he might hurt himself.

Bell boots can also be used to protect the knees on horses who tend to strike a knee with the opposite foot or leg when turning around. I position the bell boot upside-down, above the splint boot.

I usually use skid boots when I'm going to make a serious stop, whether I'm schooling or competing. I have different types, including some that provide support for the ankles and protection for the inside of the legs, and also allow the horse to slide without burning his fetlocks. These boots also help prevent sand and dirt from getting inside them, which can irritate the horse.

However, some skid boots are designed to allow sand and dirt to immediately fall through them.

All leg boots should be cleaned by brushing or washing after every use. This removes any dirt or sand that could irritate the horse, and also helps the boots last longer.

I never use leg wraps on a horse when I'm riding him, and I don't believe anyone should unless he's an expert on wrapping legs. But someone who is skilled at wrapping legs will know how to wrap them so they stay on and apply uniform pressure,

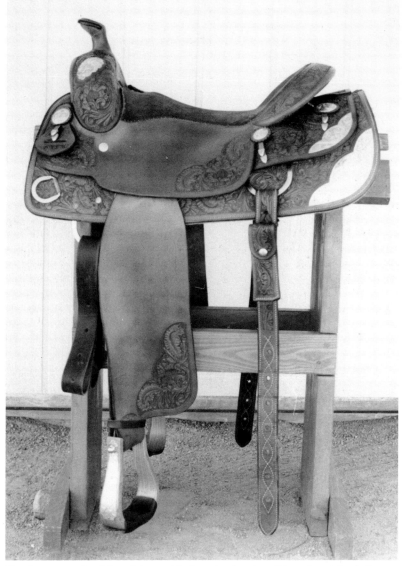

Here's an example of the reining saddle I use for showing. It has silver trim, half-breed tooling, and Nettles laminated-wood stirrups.

and will not injure a tendon or ligament or allow dirt to get under them.

Shoeing

Shoeing the front feet of a reining horse is not unlike shoeing any other western horse. I like the toes to be short, with some height to the heels. I like the shoe to

I want to keep shoeing fairly simple, and most of all, ensure that my horses stay sound.

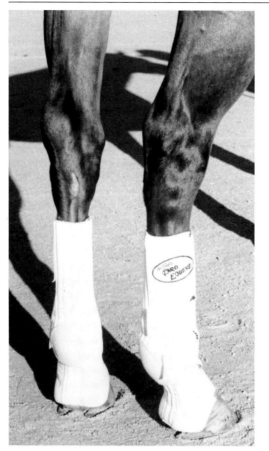

One type of a combination rear protective boot and skid boot.

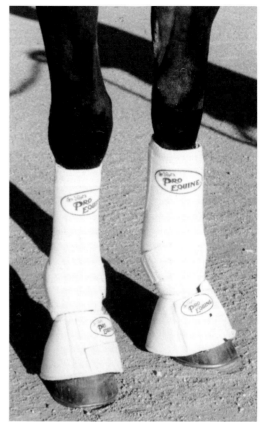

Bell boots and protective leg boots for the front legs.

extend slightly behind the heel to protect the bulb, and to be wide enough to prevent contraction of the heel.

Sometimes a horse will strike the heels of the front feet with the back feet. When this happens, we might put half-round shoes on the front feet, or square off the toes so the feet break over faster.

I don't like to do a lot of corrective trimming, and ideally I like the bottom of the hoof trimmed flat. The reason why? I don't want to disrupt the line of concussion that goes through the column of bones in the leg. If a horse's foot lands flat, it should assist in keeping the horse sound.

The sliding shoes I use are 1 to 1¼ inches

wide, and the trailers come almost straight back to protect the heels and to allow the horse the maximum surface on which to slide. I also have the toe edge of the sliders rasped or ground so the toe doesn't dig into the dirt during the beginning of the stop.

If a horse is having a problem stopping, such as splaying out, not tracking straight, not stopping equally on both legs, or digging into the ground too much, I'll slide him a few times to lay down some tracks. Then the shoer and I will study the tracks to determine what adjustment in the shoes the horse may need to help him.

Checking the wear pattern of used sliders can also help us determine any correction needed.

I'm not going into too much detail on shoeing a reining horse because this subject could make a book itself. I'll summarize by saying that I want to keep shoeing fairly simple, and most important, ensure that my horses stay sound.

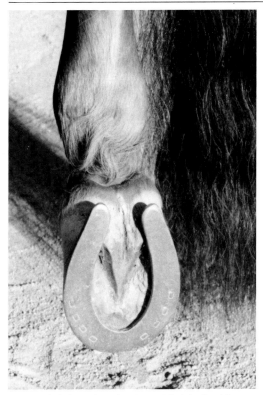

A typical sliding plate that I use. It's 1 inch wide.

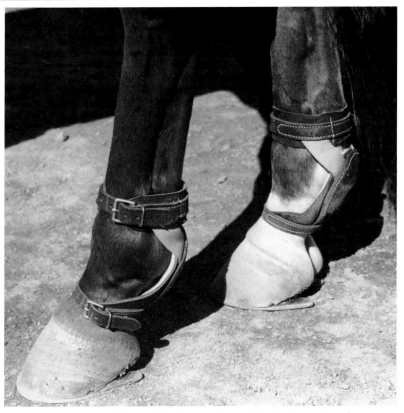

Here's another type of skid boot I like because it doesn't bind a horse. Some horses don't like restrictive boots, or boots that go up the leg higher than these do. I keep these boots loose on the bottom so if sand gets inside, it will fall right out. King's Saddlery in Sheridan, Wyo., makes these boots.

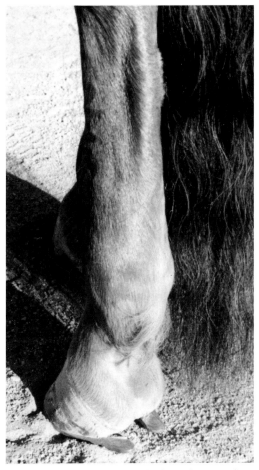

The trailers extend behind the heels, and protect the bulb of the foot.

3 FACILITIES

A round corral should be a minimum of 50 to 60 feet in diameter.

A ROUND CORRAL is a big help in starting colts, and also for working broke horses who might have particular problems. A round corral should be a minimum of 50 to 60 feet in diameter. Mine is 60 feet across, with sand footing, and it's an ideal size for starting colts. Why?

It's small enough to help control a colt who might get a little rambunctious during the breaking process, yet it's large enough so that both colts and mature horses have enough room to move freely. In round corrals that are too small, more stress is put on the legs of horses, espe-

cially young horses, because they are traveling in such small circles. Yet a 60-footer is not too big. When you're gyping (longeing) the horse free, you can easily reach him with a longe whip.

My corral is built of pipe panels and is 6 feet high. A round pen should be a minimum of 5 feet high to discourage a horse from trying to jump out, or getting his head over the top rail. The sandy footing provides good cushioning and minimizes the chances of a horse slipping and falling. Yet the sand is not so deep that it stresses a horse's tendons, ligaments, and muscles.

My arena measures 275 feet long and 120 feet wide and has a firm, flat bottom with about 2 inches of sand on top. It has pipe fencing, 6 feet high (that's a shadow of the fence on the right).

A view of our hot walker.

Photo by Kurt Markus

My round pen is 60 feet in diameter with 6-foot sides. The sides are solid wall for 4½ feet, then horizontal pipe for the top 18 inches. The 6 inches of sand footing provides good cushioning and traction and makes horses work a little harder, yet is not so deep it stresses them.

My arena is big, measuring 275 feet long and 120 feet wide. I made it large for several reasons:

1/ Several riders can school horses in it at the same time without getting in each other's way.

2/ There's plenty of width so riders can lope and gallop large circles. If an arena is so small that a rider must always lope small circles, the horse can develop the habit of dropping his inside shoulder.

3/ There's plenty of length to teach a horse to rate his speed—to accelerate and slow down when I ask him to.

4/ To make run-downs and stops, many reining patterns require the horse to gallop around the arena (rather than up and down the center). A large arena at home facilitates this practice.

In the center of the main barn are two grooming and saddling areas, just across the aisle from the tack room where we keep the equipment we use every day. **Photo by Kurt Markus**

I pay particular attention to the arena footing so that it is safe and provides a good cushion. It has a firm, flat bottom, and about 2 inches of sand on top. That gives a stopping horse something to drive through, allowing him to slide, yet also provides a cushion so he doesn't hurt himself.

Because the footing is good all over the arena, I can stop a horse anywhere; he doesn't learn any "sweet spots" where he always expects to be stopped.

Watering the arena minimizes the dust, and keeps the bottom flat and hard. A water pipe with sprinkler heads runs along the fence line and makes watering easy. After the arena is watered, we work it lengthwise with a harrow or flat drag. This works up the top 2 inches to keep the footing level and loose. We often use a large, flat drag to keep the surface even and level.

I do a lot of training on my reining track, which is a large, open area with good, even footing, with no perimeter fence. However, it does have a short length of fence on each end that we use for "fencing" when running and stopping a horse.

The biggest advantage of a track: It has no fences for the horse to rely on, or drift toward. Since it has no fences and is of a much greater size than the typical fenced arena, I can deviate my routine. For example, size of circles, direction I run, where I'm going to change leads, etc. This is a huge advantage because the horse never knows what I am going to do next. This keeps him from learning to anticipate.

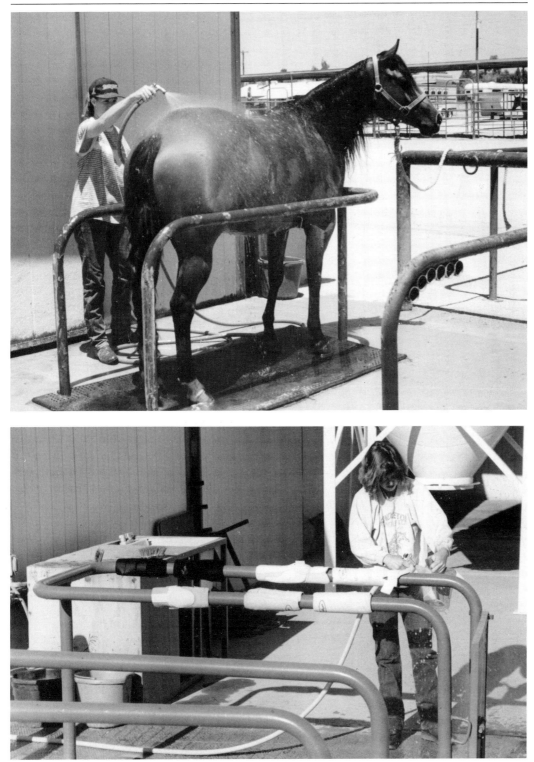

Carrie Liston is rinsing off this bay, something we do almost every time a horse is ridden. Note that the horse is not tied. We don't tie horses in the wash racks because if one happens to pull back, he can slip and fall. We simply train the horses to stand there; most of them enjoy getting a cool rinse anyway.

The pipe wash racks are also handy for washing and drying protective leg boots.

EQUITATION

A rider should sit tall, but relaxed, in order to maintain proper equitation.

BALANCE IS THE key to successfully riding a reining horse. For my students to maintain proper balance, I teach them the basic position of sitting in the center of the saddle so they are right over the middle of the horse. Both feet should be in the same position in the stirrups, with an equal amount of weight in each. This is the basic position for riding in a straight line, and in circles.

Correct posture is important. A rider should sit tall, but relaxed, in order to

Matt Kimes of Scottsdale is one of my non-pro riders. He demonstrates the basic position for good equitation in reining. Matt won the non-pro division of the 1996 NRHA Derby in Oklahoma City on one of his horses.

This is an excellent picture of Matt stopping his mare. He is sitting very still in the center of the horse, and his hand is light on the reins. He clearly demonstrates the "sit and say whoa" position that I advocate all the way through a stop.

To start the turnaround, Matt's position is good; he is turned slightly in the saddle and is in balance, not leaning. His rein hand is coming straight across the shoulders. As the mare builds speed, Matt will give her more slack.

Correct positioning of the foot in the saddle.

Matt's body and rein hand are correctly positioned over the center of the horse.

maintain proper equitation. Correct posture also gives the rider a "commanding" look—he is in charge, and not just along for the ride.

Your weight should be distributed so that you have 60 percent in your seat and 40 percent in your feet. Many riders have weak legs, and ride with almost all of their weight in their seat. This does not allow them the proper amount of leg control for balance and leg cues. These are riders who, during a stop, tend to fall forward and lose their balance point.

On the other hand, a rider who has too much weight in his stirrups tends to ride stiff-legged and push his legs extremely far forward, pinning his seat against the cantle. This is an incorrect position, not allowing the rider to absorb any of the shock correctly, or to maintain good leg position in order to use leg cues properly.

I deviate from my basic position slightly when turning a horse around and when stopping. When turning a horse around (spinning), I twist my upper body slightly into the turn and keep my inside leg hanging straight down. My outside leg is free to move and accelerate the turnaround by using the spur behind the front cinch.

When I stop a horse, I like to get down on his back. I push my weight down in the middle of the saddle; I do not lean back excessively nor fall back. I am careful to sit right in the middle of the saddle so I don't put more weight on one hind leg than the other.

When I'm making a rundown and ask the horse to stop, I sit down and say whoa, melting into the saddle. I keep my shoulders straight, but break at the waist to lower my center of gravity. I actually ride somewhat behind the motion during the run and in the stop. The horse should gradually build speed during the run, and be running "uphill" to the stop so he can more easily get his hindquarters under him to slide. On a good-stopping horse, if the rider doesn't bounce, the horse usually doesn't bounce.

Riders who tend to fall back when stopping are those who tend to overpull, using the shoulder to pull instead of the hand and arm.

Riders who tilt forward in the stop usually tend to lean forward in the rundown, instead of sitting down and riding slightly behind the motion. Sometimes they do not have their heels down or enough weight in their stirrups either.

1/ Here is a sequence of five pictures showing Matt making a rundown and stop. Here, Matt is starting to build speed in the rundown, and is keeping the horse straight between the reins.

2/ This picture shows how Matt is riding behind the motion, continuing to drive the horse. Ideally, the mare's head should be more vertical.

3/ The horse is running straight and true, and in an uphill position, ready to stop when Matt asks her to. When in a strung-out position, a horse cannot readily stop. Note that the mare's position in this photo is almost identical to her position in the previous photo.

4/ Matt has dropped his weight into the saddle and said whoa to ask the mare to stop. Note that Matt's rein hand has scarcely moved. Instead, the mare reached out with her nose and took the slack out of the reins until she felt Matt's steady hand.

When you ask the horse to stop, your hand should not move more than 6 inches back.

Throughout the reining pattern, I try to ride very quietly. I don't rock forward or back, let my elbows flop, let my hands move around, or let my legs swing. Many riders are not aware of how much their legs or hands move. Sloppy equitation can give the horse confusing signals, and detracts from the overall picture of your run that the judges see.

A good way to check out your position is to watch videotapes of your runs. You may be surprised to see that you are doing things you are not aware of.

Hands

Your basic hand position is approximately 2 inches above the saddle horn, and slightly forward. When you neck-rein the horse, you move your rein hand a few inches farther forward so the rein is applied about halfway up the neck. You don't want to use too much pressure on the neck rein because that will "drag" the horse into a turn rather than cue him. It will also pull his head out of position.

If a horse doesn't respond to a light rein, he needs more homework.

When you ask the horse to stop, your hand should not move more than 6 inches back. Any more than that, he's not responding properly.

There's one common mistake many a rider makes when stopping: He unknowingly pulls his rein hand back toward his hip (left hip if he has left hand on the reins;

Two views of Matt coming toward the camera. On the left he is loping a large, fast circle. On the right, a slower, more collected circle in which he is applying a little more neck-rein.

right hip if he's riding with right hand). This will cause an unbalanced stop. Riders should concentrate on pulling the rein hand straight back to their belt buckle. Although I show with my left hand on the reins, I often use my right hand when schooling to help balance my reining awareness.

In summary, a finished horse should be so responsive to the reins and your body movement that he reacts immediately to your imperceptible cues. That should be your goal in training and riding a reiner.

Matt shows correct positioning at the gallop. His rein hand is quiet and light, and the mare is responding to the bridle properly. Note the slack in the inside rein. Judges like to see this.

McKenzie Merrill, Purcell, Okla., is another non-pro rider. She shows excellent positioning here on Seven S Catalpa while winning the $2,000 added non-pro reining in Tucson, March 1996.

Photo by Pennau

5 BREAKING

If you do a bad job of breaking and create problems, you may never get them corrected.

WE PUT A tremendous amount of emphasis on starting colts correctly because the foundation lays the groundwork for everything we will teach them, and it will stay with them the rest of their lives. If you do a bad job of breaking and create problems, you may never get them corrected.

I have received several young horses who someone else started and made mistakes with, and I never could develop those horses to their full potential.

Since a good breaking job is so important, we prefer that a young horse not be started if he's coming to us, unless we

This young horse, just being broke, lopes with confidence in the round pen. Mike Wood, my assistant trainer, is the rider.

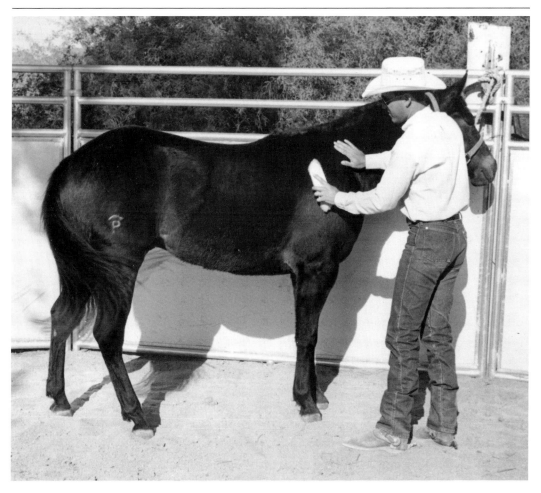

The key is to frequently tie a young colt with an unbreakable halter and unbreakable lead rope to an unbreakable post.

know the owner can do an excellent job. If the colt hasn't even been handled much, all the better. Too much early handling can make a colt cranky, as well as insensitive to cues when we begin riding him. When a colt is brought to us, all he needs is to be halter-broke, know how to lead and tie up, and be gentle enough for a little brushing.

Depending on the situation, we break some colts at our ranch, and send others to my friend Mike Kevil, whom I consider one of the best in the business at working with young horses. Mike has written his own book, *Starting Colts*, in which he describes his techniques and methods. I recommend this book, which is published and sold by Western Horseman Inc. (see the page in this book for ordering information). Therefore, I am only going to touch on a few of my breaking philosophies in this book.

The first thing we do with a colt is to make sure he will tie up without pulling back. I think that 90 percent of getting a colt easy to handle is getting him to stand quietly when he's tied. The key is to frequently tie a young colt with an unbreakable halter and unbreakable lead rope to an unbreakable post. That teaches him patience, and that he can't get loose. He should always be tied high (above his eye level) to lessen the chance of injury to his neck if he pulls back when resisting being tied.

Horses who are tied low can pull their necks down, which is a serious, usually permanent injury. A horse with a pulled-down neck usually carries his neck low, with his head to one side.

The horse should also be tied with a quick-release knot or snap so he can be untied quickly if he loses his footing and falls while resisting.

When a colt is ready to be saddled for the first time, Mike longes him to get him relaxed.

We tie a colt in the round corral and spend time brushing and handling him and picking up his feet. The latter is very important so he learns to stand quietly for the horseshoer. We also get him accustomed to having his whiskers and bridlepath clipped, but not his ears. We never clip out the ears until a horse is ready to show.

First Saddling

When a colt is ready to be started under saddle, we first longe him to get him relaxed. Then we either tie him to a post or have an assistant hold him. We sack him out with a saddle pad or blanket, rubbing him all over with it until he's no longer afraid of it anywhere on his body.

When we are ready to saddle him, we adjust the cinches to what we think will be the correct lengths, and lay them, together with the right stirrup, over the seat of the saddle. We ease the saddle on the colt, and the assistant moves to the right side, going behind the horse, to carefully lower the cinches and stirrup.

We cinch him up easily (not too tight), but if the colt looks like he's going to blow up, we go right ahead and cinch him up snug. No way do you want a colt half-cinched to rear or jump and have the

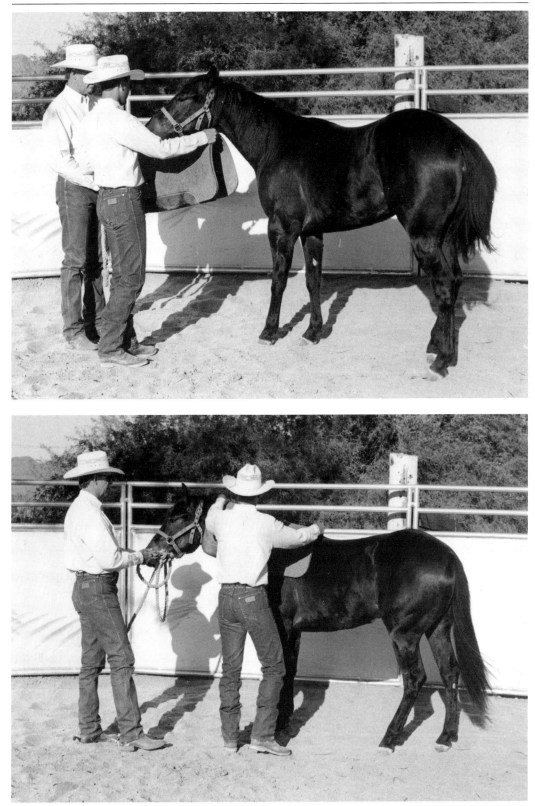

We generally use two people for the first saddling. I'm holding the colt while Mike introduces the saddle pad, letting the colt smell it.

We like to slide the pad up and down the neck and back. When sacking a spooky colt, we use an old double Navajo. Because it's softer and flops more than this pad, it does a better job of sacking out.

Introducing the saddle.

Mike lifts the saddle and carefully eases it down on the back.

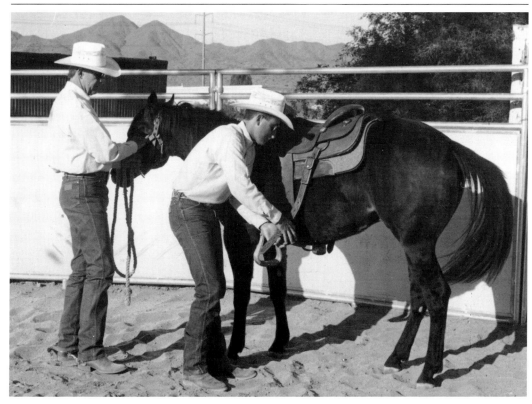

Mike doesn't cinch up too tight initially, unless the colt looks like he's going to blow up. Then he cinches snugly enough to keep the saddle in place if the colt does come uncorked. It's important that both handlers stay on the same side. Then if the colt does explode, both handlers can leave in the same direction to get out of the way.

saddle slide under his belly. Usually a colt will stand and let us cinch him to what I call medium-snug, meaning the saddle is not going to slide under his belly or fall off if he does jump.

We pull the back cinch up, leaving it an inch or so from his belly. We don't want it snug against his belly right now, but it shouldn't be so loose he could stick a hind foot in it if he bucks and pitches.

We move him off by leading him in a turn. Most of the colts we start are pretty well broke to lead, and if one does get excited about being saddled, he's not going to jerk free and run off.

We walk him a little way, take the cinch up another notch, slap the fenders against his sides, and rub on him. If the colt is nervous, we tie him up and let him stand and think awhile. With the relaxed colt, we immediately start longeing him with a longe line or rope; we do not turn him loose. We like to keep control of the colt in case he gets scared, or wants to buck. We don't want him to learn to buck, and if he starts bucking, we pull him to a stop.

Some colts will break and run blindly from fear, and will possibly injure themselves. We don't want that to happen, so we pull them to a stop, and quiet them. When they have relaxed, we ease them out again on the line, and try it again.

Once the colt will longe quietly with the saddle on, at the walk, trot, and lope, we quit for the day. But while we are longeing him, we start using the word *whoa* when we want him to stop. By using this verbal command, and tugging lightly on the line, we urge him to stop. If the colt becomes confused because he hasn't learned the word whoa yet, we pull on the line and step toward the front of the colt, making him stop and turn toward us. This starts building the foundation for learning what

47

Before tightening the cinch a little more, Mike leads the colt off in a turn. After walking the colt a little way, Mike takes the cinch up another notch.

If the colt is relaxed, Mike starts longeing him, keeping him on a line so he can be controlled should he get scared and want to buck or run off. We don't want colts to learn to buck. If one does start bucking, we pull him to a stop.

We start teaching a colt the meaning of whoa when he's on the longe line. Here, Mike has said whoa and is pulling on the line. He's also stepping toward the head of the colt and will block his path with the whip.

Here, Mike is asking the colt to reverse direction. After the colt has been longed both ways and stopped a few times, we put him up.

49

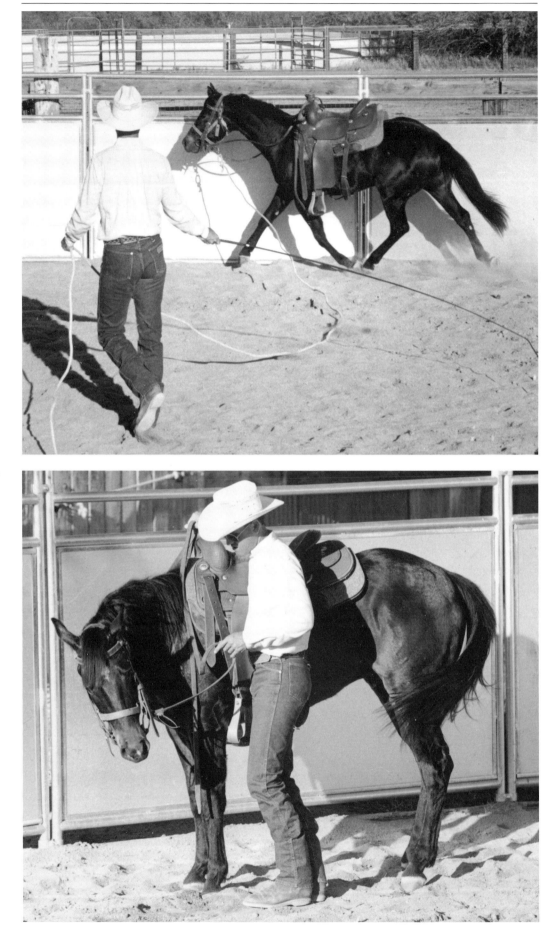

In the colt's second session, he is again sacked out, saddled, and longed, this time with a snaffle bridle over the halter. The longe line is snapped to the halter, and the reins are tied to the saddle horn with a lot of slack. Note also the slack in the longe line so it's not pulling the colt's head to the inside. But Mike is careful not to let the colt step over the longe rope.

Now Mike begins teaching him to respond to a direct pull on the reins, first on one side, then the other.

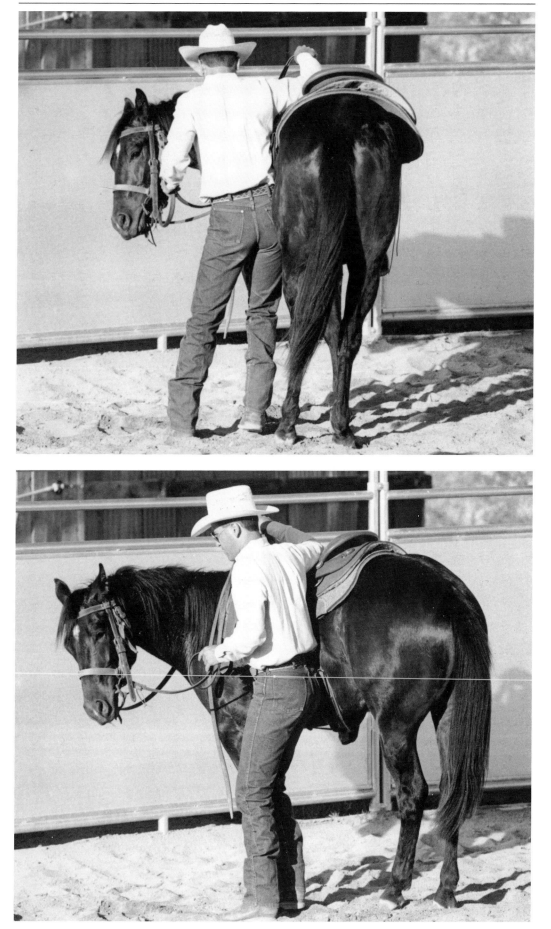

1/ Here is a sequence of three photos showing how Mike makes the colt move forward while responding to a pull on the left rein. Note how Mike is using his hip to make the colt move.

2/ Mike keeps pushing his hip into the colt to make him step around, while keeping plenty of slack in the right rein.

3/ The colt has come about halfway around in response to gentle pulls.

We do this until the colt understands to follow the pull with his head.

the word whoa means, which is so important, and which will be incorporated into the rest of his training.

In the second session, we sack him out again, saddle him, put a snaffle bridle on him (over the halter) and longe him to get the kinks out. Then, while standing next to the colt by the saddle, we pull the direct rein, bending the head and neck toward us. We repeat this on the other side. We do this until the colt understands to follow the pull with his head. Then we stand next to the colt, nudge him in the belly with a hip or knee, or cluck to him, to make him

move forward while continuing to follow the pull of the rein.

After he accepts this, we tie his head around with the rein, to the rear D-ring of the saddle or to his tail. We tie the rein so the horse is bending his neck about 90 degrees. We leave the colt in the round pen so he is free to walk around. Not only does he learn to follow the rein, but he also learns to bend his neck and body with the correct arc; he bends his neck from the base up. Later, when we get on him, he knows pretty well what we want when we pull a rein. We leave him tied around for about 30 minutes in each direction.

If the colt is not accepting the snaffle well—chewing on it or throwing his head—we put a snaffle on him (with no reins) in the stall, and let him live with it in his mouth for a few hours a day. He eats and drinks with it. That usually solves the problem.

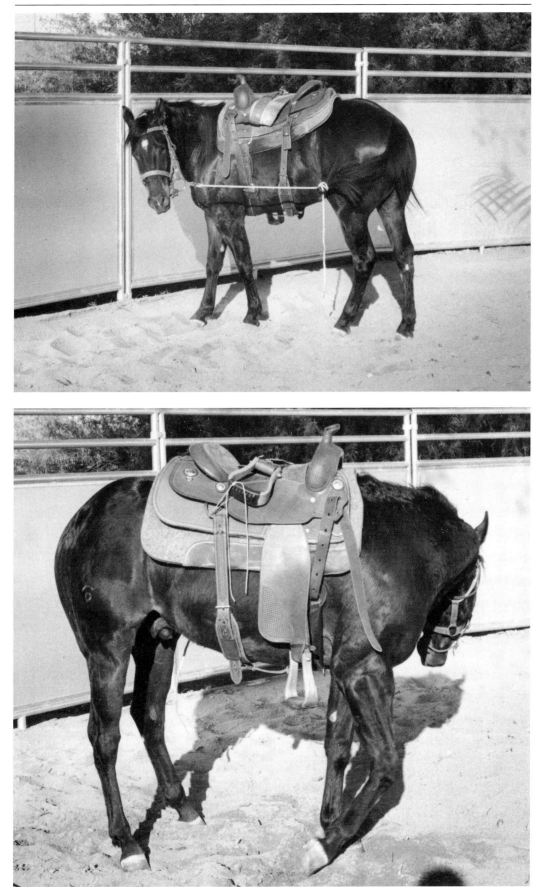

After the colt understands how to respond to the pull of the rein, we tie his head around. This develops his flexibility and further teaches him to follow the pull of the rein. If you simply tie his head around first, without teaching him how to respond to the pull of the rein, he might fight it and scare himself. The head can be tied to the rear D-ring or his tail.

When a colt's head is tied around, we tie up the stirrup on that side so the colt can't bite the stirrup and get it caught in his mouth. This can result in a real wreck.

When we first drive a colt, one person leads him. This calms the colt and gives him security.

Driving

On the third day, if things are going well, we drive the colt. We tie the stirrups together and run the driving lines from the snaffle through the stirrups. An assistant leads the colt while another person drives the colt. The assistant leads the colt to keep him under control until he is no longer afraid of the driving lines around his legs and hindquarters, and until he gets the hang of being driven.

You can drive a colt by walking straight behind him (but out of kicking range), but we usually stay more to the middle of the corral and drive the colt around the perimeter.

While the colt is being driven, he learns that a cluck and slack in the lines mean to move forward; and that whoa and light pressure on the lines mean stop. Be patient, and give the colt time to respond, and he will learn what you want. After the colt learns to move forward, turn both directions, stop, and back up with the help of the assistant, the assistant takes his lead rope off the colt and leaves the pen. Now just one person handles the colt, driving him and repeating the same maneuvers.

It might take a few days for the colt to learn to drive well, but during this process, he will become easier to handle, and generally better prepared for when a rider gets on his back.

Most colts today are much easier to handle than young horses were in years

Be patient, and give the colt time to respond, and he will learn what you want.

We run the driving lines from the snaffle through the hobbled stirrups.

Regardless of which direction the colt is moving, the person leading him always stays to the inside.

Here's a sequence of three pictures. When Mike asks the colt to turn, I step around his head, helping the colt learn to follow the pull of the driving line. Note that Mike is directing the colt's head with the left line and has plenty of slack in the right line.

Some colts are so gentle that we can ride them after just a few days of ground work, if we can stop and turn them.

past because they are better bred and usually have been handled more correctly. We just don't have the broncy horses like we used to get. On occasion, however, we receive a horse who has been spoiled through mishandling. This type of colt lacks respect for the handler and is more difficult to train than a colt who has not been handled at all.

First Ride

Some colts are so gentle that we can ride them after just a few days of ground work, if we can stop and turn them. But before getting on, we longe the colt until he's quiet; the reins are tied around the saddle horn with some slack in them. When the colt is relaxed, the rider is ready to get on.

An assistant holds the colt with the longe line, while the rider cheeks the colt and steps on slowly. With the rider sitting still and doing nothing, the assistant leads the colt until he is comfortable with the rider's weight. Then, the assistant begins longeing the colt, so the colt learns to carry the rider while moving at all three gaits. The rider stays relaxed, not giving any cues, so there's a better chance of the colt staying relaxed.

After we longe the colt sufficiently, the assistant stops the colt and removes the longe line. Now the rider pulls the colt's head a little to one side to untrack him and walk in a circle. If he's hesitant, the rider

When Mike asks the colt to back, I help the colt move back and learn what Mike wants.

This colt is driving well, without an assistant at his head. Mike asks the colt to move forward by clucking to him. He learned this cue when he was being longed.

clucks, adds some leg pressure, or slaps the colt with the rein on the outside hip to make him move. The rider walks the colt in both directions and then does the same at the trot. Depending on the colt's attitude, the rider might even ask him to lope on this first ride.

The rider doesn't use a lot of leg pressure at this stage because the colt doesn't understand it yet. Nor does the rider use spurs, or even wear them for the first few rides. The rider gradually teaches the horse to move forward in response to leg pressure by using his leg, and then a verbal command (cluck), if necessary. If leg pressure and the cluck do not work, the rider slaps the outside hind leg of the colt with a rein. As the colt learns more, he begins responding to fewer and lighter cues.

You have to be good enough a rider to follow through on what you ask the colt to do. For example, if you ask him to move forward and he doesn't respond to your legs or a cluck, you must have enough courage to reinforce your request and pop him down the hind leg with a rein. The colt might overreact, but he can't go anywhere in the round pen . . . only around and around in circles.

When Mike mounts for the first time, he cheeks the colt while I hold him with the longe line.

I lead the colt until he seems comfortable with the rider's weight.

Then I longe the colt while Mike stays relaxed and quiet in the saddle, not giving any cues.

Finally, I remove the longe line and Mike asks the colt to move off by clucking to him, and maybe applying a little leg pressure. I stay in the round pen, as if I were longeing the colt, to urge forward motion if necessary.

One whack with a rein is more meaningful than several gentle taps. Those aren't effective and will only irritate the colt.

If you continue allowing a colt to do the wrong things, such as not responding to your legs or a cluck, he'll quickly develop bad habits that can present real problems in future training.

Once the colt can walk, trot, and lope both ways, and will stop, back up, and steer, he's ready to go outside of the round pen. Depending on the colt, the time he has spent in the round pen has ranged from 3 to 10 days. We like to put a good foundation on our colts, but we don't want to stay in the round pen any longer than necessary. The colt soon becomes bored just going around in circles, so we take him to the arena or out in the desert and start the next steps in his training.

The colt moves out at a trot. Mike remains quiet, just being a passenger while the colt learns to pack Mike's weight. Note that Mike is not wearing spurs; we never do on colts for their first few rides. If a colt won't move in response to a cluck or leg pressure, the rider pops him down a back leg with the end of a rein.

Mike picks up both reins for more direct control when the colt breaks into a lope. This has been a good first ride, quiet and relaxed, which is our goal.

6 RIDING OUTSIDE

I believe this is a major reason why my horses stay fresh for years.

I AM A FIRM believer in riding horses—from green colts to finished horses—outside of the arena. When I am outside, whether in the desert or on my track, there are fewer things to distract the horse and me from concentrating on what I'm trying to teach him.

I believe you can ride a horse outside and teach him almost everything he will need to know in the show ring. Many times I will put a snaffle on my older horses, take them outside, and do different things with them, and I believe this is a major reason they stay fresh for years.

For example, I'll circle around bushes, drag a log, ride over a few obstacles and through ditches . . . anything new to keep a horse interested. Sometimes I'll even work a cow with my reiners to add purpose to their maneuvers.

If you only ride a horse in an arena, he will probably become soured and bored pretty darn fast, and then you might have to use more forceful means to get the same job done.

I realize there are many trainers who have no outside places to ride, especially in the winter months, and some still do an

Mike Wood riding a colt in the desert.

Riding outside helps a horse learn to move naturally and to travel in a straight line.

Circling a bush helps a colt learn to steer with a direct rein, and gives both colt and rider a focal point.

In these two pictures, Mike has stopped the colt and is rolling him back into the bush. As the colt learns this maneuver, Mike will ask him to do it with more speed.

This two-year-old is guiding well around the bush. His head, front feet, and rear end are all on the same arc.

outstanding job of training. My hat's off to them because I know the problems when you can ride only in an arena.

For a colt's first few rides outside the arena, we leave his head alone as much as possible. We just keep him lined out, moving forward and traveling straight. This is important because straight is the optimum for everything he will have to do in a reining pattern.

We use tall bushes to circle around, slow him down, and teach him to steer with a direct rein. Circling around a bush gives both horse and rider a focal point, which helps you make true round circles. This repetition of making true circles helps the horse learn to stay between the reins and carries over to circling in the arena.

I like to turn a colt back into a bush. I'll trot or lope around a bush several times, ask the colt to stop, and then roll him back into the bush and go the other way. This maneuver tells me a lot about a colt's suppleness and athletic ability, and also teaches

Circling around a bush gives both horse and rider a focal point, which helps you make true round circles. This repetition of making true circles helps the horse learn to stay between the reins and carries over to circling in the arena.

65

Mike is dragging part of an old railroad tie to give this colt something different to do. This is also part of our ongoing sacking-out process.

Sometimes I put a cow in my cutting pen and let a colt follow her around. This gives a colt a practical reason to "steer."

Stepping over poles keeps a colt interested and teaches him to watch where he's going.

Pasture-raised colts make much better horses when you start them under saddle than do pen-raised colts.

him a basic maneuver. And it gives him a reason to roll back correctly—to avoid brushing his head against the bush. Anytime you can give a horse a reason to do something, he learns faster.

If he can plant his hocks and feel strong using them, that tells me he'll be able to turn around and back up easily. If he can handle his front end, sweep across himself, and avoid hitting the bush, that's further proof he has potential.

Riding a colt outside teaches him to move naturally and handle himself. It helps develop his coordination and balance. He also learns how to move out and gallop. Many colts who are ridden only in an arena never have a chance to learn

these things, and their gaits can become stiff and peggy.

It's like comparing colts raised in big, rough pastures to colts raised in small pens. The pasture colts learn how to handle themselves at all speeds in different types of terrain. They make much better horses when you start them under saddle than do pen-raised colts.

We want this outside riding to be a relaxing, learning experience. This should be true for both horse and rider.

7 BACKING

Backing teaches a horse to use his hindquarters properly.

IT MIGHT SEEM out of sequence to devote an entire chapter to backing before discussing some of the more spectacular maneuvers, such as stopping or turning around. But backing is extremely important. Not only because it is a maneuver in itself that a reining horse must perform well, but also because it teaches a horse to use his hindquarters. Therefore backing plays a key role in the horse's learning how to stop, and how to turn around correctly, and to be collected in a balanced frame.

In addition, backing helps to develop the mouth, and helps put rate, or control, on the horse.

Many horses have trouble learning to back, and many riders have trouble teaching their horses to back properly. This is partly because they are not sure what to

A finished horse backs fluidly and easily, with no resistance. This picture also shows how a horse must use his hindquarters to back properly.

do when a horse refuses to back. If the horse has never had the proper foundation in training, such as learning to give to the bit, or has bad habits such as throwing his head up, the rider has added problems. But if the colt was backed when being driven from the ground, he usually has good basics for backing.

The only solution: Go back to the basics, because if you cannot get a horse to back, you are in trouble. Forget everything else until you fix this problem.

For some horses, backing is difficult because they seldom back up by themselves unless it's absolutely necessary. The added weight of a rider compounds the problem, especially on a young horse. In order to move in reverse, the horse must make his back convex; it can be hard for some colts to do this until they are more accustomed to packing the weight of a rider.

They've got to learn, however, because a reining horse must be able to use his hindquarters properly. Backing teaches him to do this.

I'll work on backing while just casually riding a colt. I'll bend his head around, then stop and ask him to back a few steps. I just pull lightly, and don't make a big production out of it. Then I'll move him on forward again, bend him a little bit, and then stop and ask him to back a few steps again. Bending his head around slightly before asking him to back keeps him limber and flexible so he is less likely to resist pressure from my light pull.

When I ask him to back, I take the slack out of both reins; then keep one hand stationary and pull lightly with the other. This uneven pressure unbalances him so it's harder for him to resist stepping back by locking (stiffening) his neck and jaw.

I don't put constant pressure on the bit, because that makes it easier for the horse to set his jaw against it. At this stage I don't like to use a see-saw motion either, because that can cause the head to go up. But I will see-saw if a horse is bulling through the bridle and I need to shake him off the bit.

Keeping one hand stationary while pulling lightly with the other might cause him to back with his body crooked. Straight, of course, is the optimum, but if a colt backs a little crooked at this stage, it's no big deal and I can realign him later.

I basically back a horse with my reins, but my legs can help the horse stay flexi-

When a colt resists backing, I'll tie his head around a little while to soften up the corners of his mouth and increase his lateral flexibility. Then before remounting, I back him from the ground.

ble while backing. I'll use my legs to push the horse into the bridle before asking him to back, to keep him straight while he backs, and to speed up his backward motion.

You don't pull on the reins harder to make a horse back faster because that can pull his head up and cause him to resist the bit.

When a horse is backing too slowly, I'll use one leg, then the other, against the belly to keep the horse's back rounded and keep him hustling backward. Sometimes I'll also pop the sides of my stirrups against his shoulders to elevate the shoulders and stimulate the front legs to push the horse back faster

If a colt does resist backing, I'll usually dismount and tie his head around for a little while. This will soften up the corners of his mouth and increase his lateral flexibility so he will handle better. When a colt handles better, he usually backs up better.

Often after I have bitted up a colt, I will back him from the ground before remounting. Standing beside the horse's

1/ This sequence depicts how I use a fence corner to help overcome a horse's resistance to backing. Here, I'm driving this young mare into the corner of the arena.

2/ As I continue to drive her, I'm trying to keep her from ducking off.

3/ As she goes into the corner, the mare starts to gather herself.

4/ Before she can brace herself physically and mentally to resist, I'll ask her to back. And she has no place to go except back.

71

5/ To ask her to back, I hold one rein steady and give a firm pull with the other, then release it quickly, and then repeat using the other hand. I'm also using slight leg pressure here to keep her straight.

6/ As she backs out, she's starting to collect herself, and bridle up.

7 & 8/ *Now she's backing well.*

left hip, I bring the right rein around the saddle horn or swells, or behind the cantle to my right hand, and the left rein straight back to my left hand. (You have to be careful if you bring the right rein behind the cantle because it could get hung up under the cantle and not release when you want it to.) Then I ask the horse to back. If I am not successful, I will bit the horse up again and try again later.

Backing the horse from the ground allows him to understand what I want, and how to do it, without having to deal with the weight of the rider.

Colts who we start from scratch rarely resist backing. The ground driving and other exercises to keep a colt flexible assures us of this.

As I have already mentioned, a colt who continues to be a problem backer needs more work on the basics.

How far do I ask a colt to back? Ideally, he should give me as many steps as I want; but right now I am more concerned that he backs freely and easily than I am with distance. If he does back well, I will ask for only three or four steps. If I feel that he will give me *only* three or four, I'll quit asking before he quits backing, or I will be determined to back a few extra steps. It's very important that he learns to keep backing until I ask him to stop; not when he wants to stop.

There's something else I do when a horse is reluctant to back: I ride him into a corner of the arena. But I don't casually walk into the corner; I'll drive him in so he stops with his body bunched up in the backing position. Then I hold one rein steady and give a firm tug with the other, release it quickly, and repeat . . . using the opposite hand. This usually works because it doesn't give the colt time to brace physically and mentally to resist backing.

Initially, as soon as he takes a couple of steps back, I immediately rein him off in another direction, go on to another corner, and repeat. After doing this a few times, he'll generally back more easily.

After he develops a simple reverse gear, I'm content if he will simply take three or four steps back readily. I'll work on the dispatch and distance later.

Occasionally I'll get a horse in who's really stubborn about backing. Often the problem stems from a rider who has pulled and hauled on the reins so much that the horse sets his jaw and refuses to give—as a defensive measure to protect his mouth. Or, maybe the horse just doesn't like to give his head.

With a horse like this, I'll bit him up to soften his mouth. I'll tie each rein straight back to the D-rings, and adjust them so that when the horse brings his nose in to the vertical, he gets slack in the reins—and relief from the pressure. While he's bitted up, I turn him loose in the round corral or arena where he can move around and we can keep an eye on him.

The average horse will usually pull on the reins only so long before he learns to come off the pressure by himself and give his head. Then he'll be a lot easier to back.

This would be a good time to mention that if the horse continually resists pressure on the reins by throwing his head up or otherwise fighting the pressure, have a veterinarian or equine dentist check his teeth and mouth. He could have wolf teeth or other dental or mouth problems. If he doesn't, at least you will know it's a training problem, or perhaps a problem with your technique.

After I've ridden a colt about 60 days, I start asking him to back farther and more quickly. My goal is to have him immediately start to back as soon as I pick up the reins and pull back lightly. I don't mean run backwards, but to back promptly and smoothly with his head in the correct position, his mouth shut, and his hindquarters under him.

I start this new program by picking up both reins and taking the slack out of them, then adding tension to both reins. If the colt doesn't come back readily, I'll pull one rein harder than the other. This might raise his head somewhat, but occasionally some things must be temporarily altered to correct others. My objective is to make him move back faster. If he comes back pretty good, I'll drop the reins and let him stand a moment.

Then I'll ask him again. I'll pick up both reins, and if he doesn't want to come back with dispatch, I'll pull one rein harder. I'll pull straight back toward my hip, while keeping firm tension on the other rein.

If the horse continually resists pressure on the reins by throwing his head up or otherwise fighting the pressure, have a veterinarian or equine dentist check his teeth and mouth.

74

1/ This is another sequence showing the same mare backing. Here, she's relaxed and definitely not collected!

2/ After walking her forward into my hands, I've asked her to back—slowly at first.

3/ *I'll shake the reins so she won't pull on my hands.*

4/ *I can use my legs against her belly or slap her shoulders with the stirrups to encourage her reverse motion.*

5/ *Now she's backing freely and lightly.*

When I pull, it's a give-and-take situation. Putting more tension on one rein keeps the colt a little more relaxed and off balance so he will be less likely to take hold of the bit and resist. But I am not see-sawing the reins.

If a colt is very resistant to backing and wants to be extremely stiff in the front legs, neck, and shoulders, you shouldn't try to overpower him by *pulling* him backwards. Try to make his legs move . . . don't just stand there and fight him.

Never pull hard with two hands against a horse that has braced himself; that will become a pulling contest that you will lose. Instead, I would turn the horse off to one side and leg him to go forward. As he's moving forward, I take the slack out of the reins, and pull one rein, then the other rapidly, shaking the horse off the bit; it's a rapid see-saw motion. This is abrupt and the horse should stop his forward motion quickly.

At that point I give him slack in the reins; he begins to realize that going forward is not such a good idea. After he stands, I'll pick up the reins and lightly ask him to back. If he backs, that's fine, and I'll give him some slack to reward him. But if he resists again, I'll repeat what

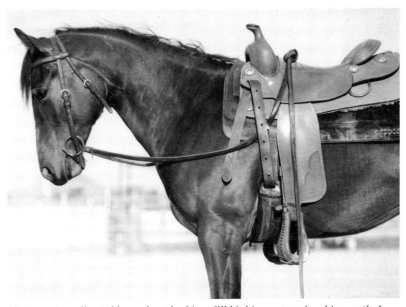

If a horse is really stubborn about backing, I'll bit him up to soften his mouth. I bring each rein straight back to the dees and tie them off. The length of the reins is adjusted so when the horse brings his nose in to vertical position, as shown, he puts slack in the reins and gets relief from the pressure.

1/ In this sequence I show how to correct a horse not backing up straight. Here, his rear end is drifting to his left.

2/ Rather than kicking or spurring with my left leg to move his rear end over, I have simply used my reins to move the horse's front end over to realign him. Using my reins instead of my legs results in less resistance later.

I call the brick-wall method. Pretty quick, he learns that going forward is not fun; it's easier to just back up.

I also want the colt supple, so he backs fluidly and freely as soon as I pick up the reins and pull lightly. I don't want him scared, with his body tense and stiff. To encourage him to move back a little faster, I might nudge him in the belly with my heel or spur, and I might also cluck to him.

When I cluck to my horses, they know that means I want more out of them. But I never cluck until the horse is already doing what I have asked. For example, I don't cluck for more speed in a back-up until the horse is already backing. It's the same with nudging him with my heel to ask for more speed.

As I have already mentioned, backing

teaches a colt how to use his hindquarters to stop and turn around. Teaching him to back on a fairly light rein is also helping to develop his mouth. He is learning to *give*—to drop his head and tuck his nose in—as soon as I pick up the reins.

Backing also helps put rate, or control, in a horse. In no way is a good reining horse anything like a barrel horse or any other speed horse who runs wide open (although even speed-event horses must have some rate in them). A reining horse is not running against time; he's always moving at a controlled speed, even in rundowns prior to stopping. Rate in a reining horse is very important, and I start putting rate in a colt when I'm backing him up. How?

As he backs, he's 1/ giving to pressure from the bit and 2/ making his back convex. Later when I'm galloping him and pick up the reins, he's already learned to

3/ *I am using a combination of rein and leg to straighten him.*

4/ *Now he's straight.*

Mike Wood is backing this 2-year-old on our track. The colt is a little over-flexed and isn't using his hindquarters properly yet.

When a colt resists backing, it helps to back him from the ground.

give his jaw and slow down. That's rate. As soon as he does this, it shortens his stride, makes him arch his back, and, with the aid of my legs, gets him to galloping under himself in a collected manner. Then he's in position to stop properly.

At no time when I pick up the reins to slow the horse do I want him to "hollow out"; that is, for his front end to come up while his back goes down. I want just the opposite: the head to drop (give), hindquarters to drive up under him, and the back to round. This is the basis of collection.

As the colt learns to back with dispatch, I pay strict attention to keeping him straight. Two keys to this are keeping the reins absolutely even, so he's getting equal pressure on both sides of his mouth; and keeping my weight equally distributed. It's more difficult for him to back straight if I am leaning to one side or sitting off center.

In theory the horse should back straight if the reins are even and his body is straight when he starts. But he may get a crook in his body after a few steps. To correct this, I like to move his front end over to align it with the rear end. For example, suppose his rear end is drifting to the right. Using a combination of direct and indirect rein, I'll move his front end over to the right.

Or, I might walk him forward a few steps, realign his front with his rear, and start over. With a colt who persistently backs crooked, I might position him alongside a fence. Once he teaches himself to back straight along a fence, it's a lot easier for me to keep him straight when we are away from the fence.

On a more advanced horse who backs crooked, I can use my legs to straighten him. Say, for example, the rear end is drifting to the left. I can use my left leg to move the rear end over to the right; or I can use my right leg to bump the right shoulder over to the left. I'm always aware of how much pressure I have on each rein.

I realign colts by using more rein than leg until they better understand leg pressure. A green colt might move *into* my leg instead of away from it, compounding the problem.

Here are two photos showing a finished horse backing straight and fast on a light rein. Note how he is using his hindquarters.

8 BODY CONTROL AND SUPPLING

Suppling refers to making the horse's body more flexible, which in turn allows us to have more control of the body.

FOR A HORSE to excel in any event, but especially reining, the rider must have control of the horse's total body. Having control of just one part of the body without control of the others is not very effective. For example, suppose you have control of the head and neck, but not of the shoulders, ribs, and hindquarters. It would then be very difficult to lope circles properly, change leads, make turn-arounds and straight run-downs, and even stop correctly.

Suppling refers to making the horse's body more flexible, which in turn allows us to have more control of the body. If, for example, a horse will not flex his neck to the right, it would be very difficult to control him because the rider could not turn him to the right without great difficulty.

By this stage, we have already done

After doing bending, backing, and leg control exercises, this horse is flexing very nicely in response to very light rein pressure. I'm riding him with draw reins.

some suppling exercises with a colt (in chapter 5). The work we do now to develop body control will, at the same time, develop even more suppleness.

We first get control of the head and neck with the bit and reins; followed by control of the rest of the body with our legs. To obtain the latter, we use a combination of our legs and reins to get the horse to "stand up" between the reins so he cannot drop one shoulder or the other. (A horse is said to "drop a shoulder" when he carries one lower than the other. It can happen when the horse is moving straight, just as a person can drop one shoulder while walking in a straight line. But it's more apt to happen in circles and while turning.)

Once we get control of the head, poll, neck, shoulders, and ribs, the hindquarters will follow, just like a caboose.

Our colt is in grade school now. I have control of his head, he is supple, can flex vertically and laterally, and can back well. Now I start putting some leg pressure on him. I use leg control to help teach him to pick up his leads, change leads, move forward or back in a straight line, and turn around correctly.

I put leg on my colts fairly easily. While walking or trotting, either outside or in the arena, I pick up both reins and use them to keep the colt's body straight while I apply leg pressure on one side, trying to get the colt to move sideways. What I'm trying to teach him is a two-track. Actually, it's a leg yield, not a two-track. In a two-track, the horse looks into the direction he is moving; in a leg yield, he doesn't. But most western trainers refer to a leg yield as a two-track, so that's what we'll call it.

I two-track a colt just enough to get more control of his body, and to help develop his suppleness and coordination.

Suppose I want to two-track to the left. I take the slack out of my reins and hold the front end straight. I press my right leg against him, and maybe bump him with my right heel if necessary. (I do just the opposite to two-track to the right.)

The horse's natural reaction will be to turn his head to the right, but I don't want him to. So I put just enough tension on the left rein to keep his head fairly straight. He can turn it a degree or two to the right, but no more.

Two-tracking is just one maneuver I use to help gain more control of a horse's body, and to develop suppleness and coordination. This horse is two-tracking well to his left, with his body almost straight.

83

1 & 2/ *In teaching the two-track (leg yield) to the left, I take the slack out of both reins to keep the front as straight as possible. I apply pressure with my right leg behind the front cinch and keep my left leg well away from the horse. Because of the forward motion, the horse will cross his outside leg over the inside. He crosses over first in front, and then behind.*

1 & 2/ In a two-track to the right, I use my left leg and keep my right leg well away from him. I continue to hold the front end in-line with the rear.

Once a colt has learned to move away from my leg in a two-track, I teach him to side-pass. I position him facing a safe, high fence that he cannot get his head over. I am using draw reins to teach this horse to stay in frame rather than resist and throw his head.

It's important to be patient, repetitious, and persistent.

Side-Pass

Once the colt has the idea to move away from my leg, the next step is to make him more responsive. I do this by teaching him to side-pass. Some people teach the side-pass first, then the two-track. But I prefer to teach the horse to yield to my leg while he's moving forward; this gives him more time to adjust, and gives him somewhere to go when moving away from my leg pressure.

To teach the side-pass first, you almost have to force the horse to go straight sideways by using strong leg pressure. This can cause a lot more resistance because the colt doesn't understand. He will probably react by switching his tail, throwing his head, trying to back up, or trying to move into my leg instead of away from it. Asking him to move away from my leg while he's moving forward minimizes or eliminates such resistance.

To side-pass, I position the horse facing a high fence, one that he can't get his head over. To go to the left, I do the same thing as before: Pick up both reins and hold his front straight, and press my right leg against him. I keep my left leg well away from him.

The fence prevents the horse from moving forward. I've got to show him that he can get away from the pressure by moving to the left. As soon as he takes just one step, I stop and release my rein and leg pressure to reward him. If he doesn't move, I increase the pressure from my right leg, and maybe boot him with my heel a few times if necessary. The fence will be there to contain him, and he should move sideways.

It's important to be patient, repetitious, and persistent. If the colt wants to move into your leg by side-passing to the right, hang in there. Don't give up. Pretty soon he will figure it out if you continue the correct cues.

Try to prevent mistakes when teaching a horse to side-pass and two-track. For example, keep your non-pressure leg well away from the horse. Some riders unknowingly apply pressure from that leg, which confuses the horse. Stick your non-pressure leg well out to the side—exaggerate if you have to—and keep it motionless.

Don't ask the horse to side-pass too far too soon. As soon as he takes just one or two steps, it's important to release the pressure and reward him. This tells him he is doing what you are asking. If you don't reward him for just one or two steps, and you keep pressuring him to move, you are sending a mixed message that will confuse him and possibly make him rebel. As in all aspects of training, don't ask for too much too soon.

When you ask the horse to side-pass, don't allow him to back up. This happens when the rider is too forceful with the reins or doesn't use enough leg pressure. If he does try to back up, use your legs to move him forward.

Arc Drills

There are several drills I use as another method to teach the horse to move away from my legs while I develop more shoulder control. In the first drill, start by walking a 10-foot circle to the left, keeping the horse in a slight left arc where you can just see the corner of the inside (left) eye. If the horse drifts out and doesn't maintain the path of the circle while walking in a collected manner, I increase the arc by pulling the head toward my left leg. I do this by pulling to my left hip, using the tug-and-release method. This limbers the neck and poll so that it's easier for the horse to maintain the arc.

You can also use your left leg to help. By applying light pressure with that leg, you are basically bending the horse around your inside leg.

A more advanced drill: Continue with the arc to the left, adding more left leg, while making the horse move to the right

Side-passing to the right. Using the fence as a barrier to forward motion allows me to be lighter with my hands and concentrate on the horse's motion and straightness.

87

REVERSE ARC DRILL

(A sequence of five.)

1/ I have been walking approximately 10-foot circles to the left, making sure the horse is following his head with his body in a slight arc to the left. Here, I am exaggerating the arc, but am starting to change directions and move to my right. Note how the horse is bent around my inside leg.

2/ The hindquarters are scarcely moving while the shoulder leads the turn to the right. Note how the left rein is against the neck and the right rein maintains the direction as the horse moves away from my left leg. We are moving from left to right. Reversing the arc improves the horse's flexibility and helps me develop more leg control.

3/ Continuing to move in a right-hand circle in a reverse arc. The horse is relaxed and giving well to my left leg.

4/ *After completing a 360-degree reverse arc, I can feel the horse's body relax and become more supple. Now I'm changing my hands into a turning position and allowing the horse to turn left.*

in a side-passing motion, with just a little forward motion.

To go a step farther, you can maintain the arc to the right while slowing the hind feet down, pushing the neck and shoulder more to the left, and keeping the front end moving. You are turning to the right while maintaining an arc to the left, using only as much leg pressure as necessary. This is a counter arc or reverse arc maneuver.

After all of these suppling maneuvers, the horse should be more willing to maintain the left arc and give (yield) his head to the left rein. So by releasing your left leg now, and turning back to the left, the horse should willingly turn in a proper arc. You are almost doing a turn-around.

Back-Around Drill

I also like to do what I call a back-around drill. I start by walking a collected circle 8 to 10 feet in diameter. I want the nose, front feet, and hind end all on the same arc. Once the horse is doing this well, I jog the same-size circle. When I'm comfortable with my horse's flexibility at the jog, I stop. Then I turn 180 degrees (a half-

5/ *The horse comfortably crosses his front legs over in a correct turn to the left. The suppling achieved in the reverse arc drill makes it easier for the horse to turn correctly.*

89

BACK-AROUND DRILL

(A sequence of ten.)

1/ *I start by walking a circle approximately 8 to 10 feet in diameter. The horse should follow his head with his neck, shoulders, and hindquarters on the perimeter of the circle, with no resistance. Once this is accomplished I circle at the jog, as shown here.*

2/ *After the horse jogs several circles correctly, I stop on the perimeter.*

3/ I make a half-turn to the inside of the circle, maintaining the same arc. In this case, an arc to the right.

4/ During the half-turn, I keep the head fairly vertical and push the shoulders around to my right.

5/ The hind legs should stay on the perimeter line. This young horse is maintaining good form.

6/ After completing the half-turn, I continue to keep the arc to the right and start to back up.

7/ I back around the same circle that I previously walked and jogged.

8/ I can use my right leg to keep the horse on the perimeter line, and to assist in keeping him flexible.

9/ Backing a circle in the correct arc makes the horse become more supple and collected. This photo shows how far I have tipped the head to the outside.

10/ After this horse is backing around well, which he's doing here, I make a half-turn into the arc (or to the right), then walk out. This exercise develops more suppleness in your horse and helps you in training him to back, turn, and collect himself.

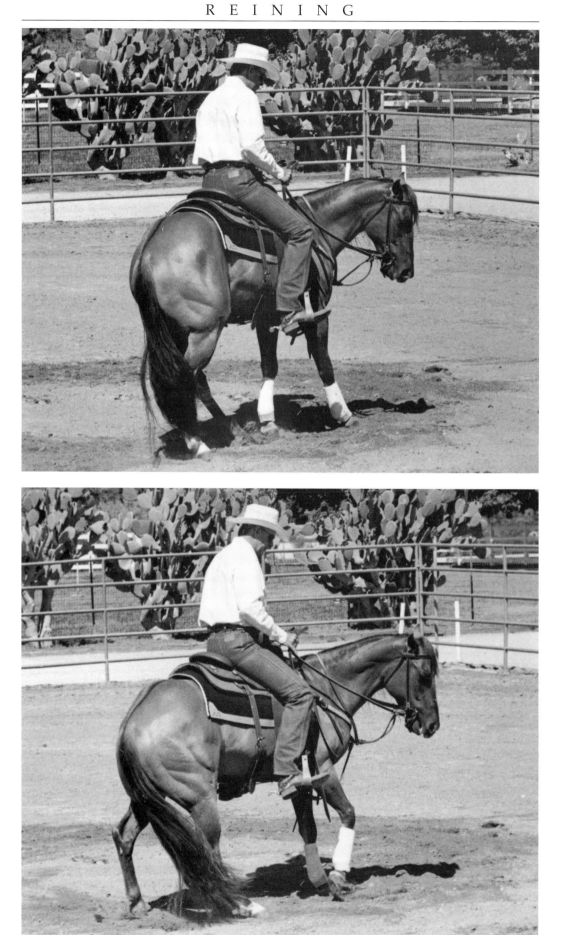

1/ Using a bush, tree, or cone as a focal point can help you make perfect circles, whether going forward or backing up. This colt is flexing his poll, lifting his shoulders, and bending his loin as he backs around in a right arc.

turn) and begin backing in a circle. I back in the same tracks I made while going forward, and I maintain the same arc.

I keep the circle as symmetrical as possible. Backing around a cone, bush, or tree gives me a focal point, which helps me back in perfectly round circles.

Suppose I'm backing the horse in an arc to the right. When he is backing freely, staying collected, and in the correct arc, I make a half-turn to the right (to the outside of the circle), then walk forward onto the path of the circle.

In this back-around drill, I have walked and jogged in a right arc, stopped and made a half-turn to the right, backed in a right arc, and made another half-turn to the right. This makes the horse learn to do everything better to the right . . . and to the left when I repeat the drill in that direction.

This is an excellent drill not only for horses, but also riders. When you can back in a perfect circle, you have very good control of your own body as well as that of your horse. And it is another step in making your horse really supple and broke.

The term *broke* means different things to different riders, but in the reining horse world, it means you have total control of the horse's entire body.

2/ Here, the colt has good form and is backing freely. Next, I will make a half-turn to the right, onto the original perimeter of the circle. I let him relax a few minutes or work on something else, then repeat the back-around drill to the left.

9 CIRCLES

If you have a solid circling horse, you will probably have a solid lead-changing horse.

CIRCLES ARE an integral part of the reining pattern, as well as part of the foundation I like to put on a colt. In a reining pattern, circles are more than just a means to show that the horse can change leads.

Circles reveal if the horse is a good mover and if he has the ability to follow his nose, stay between the reins, rate his speed by showing a distinct difference between his small, slow and large, fast circles, and travel on the correct lead in a pleasing style.

When performed correctly, circles are pretty to watch, and both horsemen and judges appreciate them because of the work that goes into achieving them.

I stress circles in my training program for two reasons: 1/ Judges pay as much attention to them as they do the other parts of a reining pattern, and 2/ from a circle you can build into other maneuvers. You can work on stopping and backing, turning around, and rolling back. You can teach a horse to rate his speed—to move faster or slow down. If he wants to move too fast, it's easier to teach him to slow down and relax while he's moving in circles rather than on a straightaway.

A finished horse circling nicely and staying between the reins.

Loping in a right circle, this gelding is in good form. His nose is just enough to the inside of the circle so I can barely see his eye. His head, front feet, and hind feet are on the same track. Notice that I have slightly more weight in my outside stirrup. I am sitting tall and balanced—not leaning or dropping my shoulder to the inside of the circle.

I am lightly guiding the horse in a big, fast circle. My hand is over the middle of the neck and there is slack in the reins. The horse is staying between the reins and he has a well-broke look about him.

If you have a solid circling horse, you will probably have a solid lead-changing horse. Most people should not ask a horse to change leads until he is deadset solid in his circles. I seldom ask a horse to change leads until:

1/ I can push him in and out of circles with my leg and put him wherever I want.

2/ I can point him where I want him to go, and he'll go there with his head in the correct position, on a light rein.

3/ I can rate his speed.

If I ask him to change leads before I can do those things, it can create problems, such as making him chargey. I want the circles to be correct first.

In order to circle correctly, the horse must have a slight arc to his body, but it's very slight; his nose should be to the inside just enough so I can barely see his eye. His neck should follow his nose, his shoulders should follow his neck, his back should follow his shoulders, and his hindquarters should follow his back—all on the same track. Both shoulders should be straight up, and he should be relaxed and moving on very light contact.

This body position is also the same basic position the horse will use later for more advanced work, like turning around.

A horse should not look too far to the inside of the circle with a lot of curvature to his body. This is unnatural and causes

When I ride on my track, the horse has no fences to lean on or drift toward, or gates to think about. This mare is guiding well off the outside rein, and is relaxed and happy.

when both shoulders are straight up. That allows him to make a smooth, more efficient change, and will prevent him from developing the habit of diving into his lead changes.

To start a colt on circles, I pick a tree or bush that's on level ground with good footing surrounding it. First at the trot and later at the lope, we go around and around that bush in nice, uniform circles. When circling an object, a horse has less tendency to duck to the inside, and it also gives both him and the rider a focal point. This is a big help in learning to make perfectly round circles . . . staying the same distance from the object all the way around the circle.

If you have no place to ride outside, use something like a bucket, barrel, or cone in the arena.

To keep his body positioned properly, I use light rein contact to put his head where I want it, then I ease off. When his head gets out of position, I pick up the reins again and put it back where it belongs, then ease off. I want him to learn to keep his head where I put it without my having to keep pressure on the reins.

If we are circling to the left, I want him to learn that he stays in that circle until I tell him otherwise. That's what "to stay between the reins" means. If you maintain constant rein pressure, the horse learns to depend on it or even lean against the rein. The horse doesn't know where to go. Constant pressure can also dull the mouth.

The horse needs direction and a way to respond to relieve pressure. Loosening the reins is a reward for the horse's correct response.

I use the outside rein to restrict his forward motion or rate his speed, and to keep him vertical and straight. I urge him along with my outside foot, which also serves to keep his ribs in so his body doesn't over-arc. My inside rein directs the horse in the circle and maintains the correct inside arc. I am, of course, still using the snaffle in this stage of training.

In schooling, I circle in both directions, but never so long that the horse gets bored. After maybe a half-dozen circles one way, I'll straighten out and head off to another bush and circle the other way a few times.

When I lope in circles, the horse must

his rib cage to push to the outside, making it more difficult for him to move properly and maneuver. In order to follow his nose, he will also tend to dive into his circles, which diminishes the rider's control.

Looking to the outside of the circle is also undesirable. That causes his inside shoulder to drop, which in turn diminishes the rider's control. It also makes the horse cut his circles down to a smaller size because he's leading with his inside shoulder. Excessive bend, either to the inside or outside, also makes it difficult for the horse to change leads.

He can change leads much easier when his head is straight in front of him, and

Here, I am loping a large, fast circle. I'm leaning forward just a little and have extended my rein hand up the neck. Those two subtle cues, plus verbal clucking, tell the horse I'm asking for more speed. The position of the mare is good; her neck is level, her face is vertical, and she's showing good extension.

Now I'm beginning a small, slow circle. I have stopped clucking, have relaxed, settled back in the saddle, am sitting straighter, and have brought my rein hand back. The mare has come back to me in speed, and has become more collected.

If a horse cannot make fast circles and look pretty while doing them, you must make a decision.

pick up the correct lead, but I don't make a big hassle out of it with a colt just learning. To move him into the lope from a trot, I sit down in the saddle to keep my weight in one place; steady his head with both reins, keeping his head straight in front of him or maybe slightly to the inside; bump him with my outside foot or leg; and cluck to him.

If he keeps trotting, I stop and start over, or I slap him down the outside rear leg with a rein. Don't lose your cool if you do this; just swat him and go on. If he picks up the wrong lead, I don't stop him right away because at this point I just want him to pick up the lope when I ask for it. Immediately stopping him will confuse him. The next chapter discusses leads in more detail.

Most colts are a little tense or nervous when you start them in circles, partly because they don't know what you want them to do. To relax them, lope a lot of circles of varying size and speed. You can do some of this inside the arena, but I like to do most of it outside where I can put more control on the colt because there are no fences or gates for him to rely on. Then when I do take him into the arena, it's a lot easier to make uniform circles because I have so much control on the colt.

After several weeks of loping circles, I have taught this colt how to rate his speed, keep his body straight except for a slight arc to the inside, lope different-size circles, and stay between the reins. I can also move him in and out of the circles. That means if I touch him on the neck with the right rein while we're loping a left-hand circle, he should make smaller circles and still be under complete control. When I take that rein off his neck, he stays between the reins while still loping that same-size circle. When I touch the horse with the outside rein, I also use the inside rein to keep his head positioned properly, and to help him comprehend. In other

words, I ask with the outside rein to make a smaller circle, then use the inside rein to show him what I want. At this stage, he usually will not respond to a neck-rein only.

I teach my colts to neck-rein very gradually over a long period of time—months and months. After I've been riding a colt several weeks, I lightly lay the indirect rein against his neck whenever I turn him with the direct rein. Or I do just the opposite; lay the indirect rein (neck-rein) on the neck and then pull lightly on his nose with the direct rein to help him understand what I'm asking with the indirect rein.

Gradually he learns to respond to the indirect rein, but it might be a year or so before I ever ask him to turn from the indirect rein only.

Small, Slow; Big, Fast

Reining patterns require changes in the speed and size of circles. So after a young horse is solid at galloping correct circles, it's time to refine them.

I start by speeding up slightly until I feel the horse moving freely and extending himself to move faster. I want a free, flowing motion. I don't want him running wide open, but at a speed that's faster yet still under control, while the horse remains collected.

Some horses do not have a pretty way of moving when going fast, or are rough to ride. But when you slow them down just a little, they present a prettier way of moving to the judge and are easier to ride. Because the rider often can't tell at what speed his horse looks the prettiest, have a ground person watch and advise you.

If a horse cannot make fast circles and look pretty while doing them, you must make a decision. Either go ahead and make fast circles and maybe lose a half-point or so because they aren't pretty, or gear him down so he looks prettier but isn't moving as fast. That can also cost you, but it might be worth it if you can make it up with scorching stops and turn-arounds. It's a judgment call.

Here's something else you can do: Make your small, slow circles slower than average so that when you do speed up, even if

When a horse gets chargey while galloping circles, I stop his for-ward motion and reprimand him by rolling back into the fence. In this picture I have just rolled back to the left because the colt was getting too strong on the right lead.

After the rollback, I ease him into the left lead. I lope a short distance, then stop and roll back again and immediately go into a right-hand circle. After my reprimand, he should listen to me better.

it isn't very fast, you show a distinct change in speed.

When transitioning from big-fast to small-slow, I sit up straight (I had been leaning slightly forward at the faster lope), and relax my body, getting into the rhythm of a slower lope. The horse can feel the change in my body, and that will help slow him. I also take a light hold to increase his collection, which slows his stride, and then release when he does slow.

When a colt doesn't respond to these cues to slow down. I stop, roll back, lope the other way just a few strides, then immediately stop and roll back again. This will make the horse respect what I had asked him to do, and to respond by rating his speed.

When running a pattern, I allow about three strides to slow down properly, and do it right in the center of the arena.

Suppose a horse anticipates either speeding up or slowing down as he approaches the center. I work on this at home by not asking for a change in speed until he's moving into the new circle, beyond the center. If I ask for a change of speed in the center, he might try to dive off

in the opposite direction, anticipating a lead change.

I don't practice a lot of big-fast to small-slow because it can result in a horse ducking or dropping his shoulders in the circle. Instead, I practice big-fast to big-slow.

Rollbacks From Circles

Rollbacks are an important part of training and showing a reining horse, and there's a whole chapter on them later in the book. But I want to mention here that I start building a foundation for rollbacks from the time I start turning a young horse into the fence to slow him down or to go in the opposite direction.

I also spend a lot of time backing a colt, then rolling back and loping off in one smooth motion. It's important that we teach a colt to back well and then maintain his motion in the rollback. In other words, I don't stop (while backing) and then turn. While he's still moving in his back-up, I roll him back.

This teaches the colt to use his rear end

To teach my students to make circles of equal size, I make them imagine that each half of the arena is a baseball diamond.

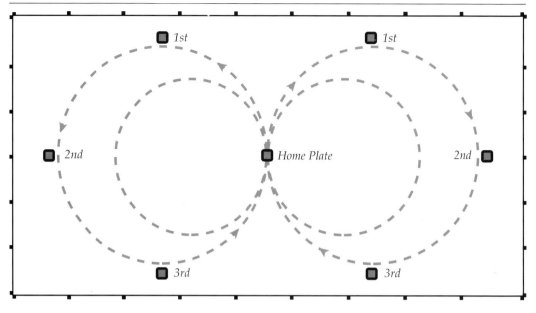

If a horse circles too fast, continually stopping and rolling back will slow him.

to turn, then push from his hindquarters while picking up the lope.

After the colt is farther along in his training, I can lay more foundation for the rollback while loping circles. When I want to change directions, I lope alongside the fence, pull his head into the fence, sit down and say whoa. Then I add pressure from my outside leg and rein to complete the rollback and head off in the opposite direction.

I do a lot of this: circle, stop, and roll back. This also helps rate the horse's speed in his circles. If he's inclined to go too fast, continually stopping and rolling back will make him think *stop,* which will slow his speed.

Problems

When I have a problem with a horse dropping his shoulder or leaning to the inside of the circle, I always go back to two hands, and school him in a snaffle. I make sure that he is well-collected and keeping his hip slightly to the inside of the circle. I want his shoulders to be up straight or, to overemphasize the point, to the outside of the perimeter of the circle

The horse's head should be straight. The more the horse wants to lean to the inside, the less arc I want to the inside. Horses have a tendency to follow their heads. So if you keep the head straight

instead of turned to the inside, the shoulders should stay straight.

I keep my outside hand low and my inside hand higher and more forward. By doing this, I can control the poll and inside shoulder. I can also ease the horse to the outside of the circle by keeping the head straight, shoulder up, and the hip slightly to the inside.

If your horse persists in dropping his shoulder, you should be aware of your position in the saddle. Many times you can correct the problem by adding more weight to the outside stirrup, and making sure that you are not dropping your inside shoulder.

Stopping a horse and turning him to the outside of the circle, one or more full turns, will also help remedy this problem.

I will also hold my inside rein steady to keep the horse's head straight. At the same time I will give a quick pull on the outside rein to direct the shoulder to the outside of the circle. That will straighten up his whole body, making him think more to the outside of the circle instead of inside. In other words, horses sometimes think about cutting the circle to make it smaller. Making him think *outside* prevents this.

Making *round* circles, and circles of equal size, is difficult for some reiners. Here's how I teach my students to make sure their right and left circles are the same size:

I make them imagine that the arena is in

102

This young horse has been dropping his inside shoulder and consequently cutting the size of his circles. To correct the problem, I raise my inside rein up while steadying the horse with my outside rein. I will also quickly pull the outside rein once or twice, which will stand both shoulders up straight.

Once the horse has straightened his shoulders up, I release the reins and allow the horse to relax in his new frame on the perimeter of the circle.

two halves, and that each half has a set of bases like a baseball diamond (see diagram), with home plate in the center of the arena.

By touching each base, the rider is ensured of an exact pattern. I also teach that the small, slow circle should be approximately half the size of the large-fast, but this depends greatly on the arena size.

Mistakes

There are several mistakes novice riders tend to make when they break their own colts. Perhaps the most common is teaching a colt to neck-rein too soon. Many riders do this by laying the indirect rein against the neck with a heavy hand, or hard pull. This can cause problems such as the horse reversing his arc, tipping his head to the outside or throwing it up. It can also cause the horse to duck and dive rather than staying between the reins. As I mentioned earlier, I'll ride a colt for months before ever using a neck-rein only.

Another mistake is allowing the colt to "string out behind" while loping. You should keep him collected, keeping his hindquarters under him. Many riders mistakenly believe that if a horse is flexed at the poll with his face vertical, he is collected, but

that's not necessarily true. He can string out behind while flexed at the poll.

To collect the horse, squeeze with your legs to drive his hindquarters up and under him. To restrict him from going faster, take a light hold of his mouth as you squeeze with your legs. This creates more of an up-and-down motion, i.e. collection, rather than stretching out and going faster.

Another common mistake when training is sticking your inside hand way out to the side to "lead" the horse in that direction, as in plow reining. That puts too much weight on the inside shoulder; you want the horse's weight shifted more toward the rear, even in circles.

What you should do is pull your inside hand straight back to your hip. This method has another advantage: It more closely resembles how you will later turn the horse with just one hand on the reins. On a finished horse, you should have complete control without moving your hand more than a few inches from the horn.

10 PICKING UP LEADS

If the horse cannot travel in the correct lead, he will have great difficulty in becoming a good performance horse.

EVEN THOUGH picking up the correct lead is simple to do, it's very important. If the horse cannot travel in the correct lead, he will have great difficulty in becoming a good performance horse, or even just a good riding horse.

Most experienced horsemen have no trouble with teaching a horse to pick up both leads, and seldom even think about it. It's just second nature for us to set up the horse to pick up the lead we want, and

we begin doing it a little bit when we first start riding the colt outside. But now it's time to get serious and refine our signals so the colt learns to instantly pick up whichever lead we ask for.

Leg pressure is a key part of this, and we've already put some leg on the colt by side-passing and two-tracking him.

You can work on leads outside, but it's easier in the arena, alongside the fence. Let's start by picking up the right lead

To excel in performance events, a horse must be able to pick up and travel in the correct lead.

1/ A sequence of four pictures showing this young filly learning to pick up her left lead. Here, we are walking down the fence. I have collected her, angled her toward the fence, and moved my hands toward the fence so her shoulders are in the position to let her hind lead start first.

2/ I have added right-leg pressure and have my left leg well away from her side.

3/ *I continue to keep her right shoulder toward the fence as her left hind leg moves forward to initiate the lead.*

4/ *She is pushing off with her left hind and now is elevating her shoulders to complete the left-lead departure.*

since most horses have more trouble picking up this lead than the left. In fact, most horses have more trouble doing everything to the right, possibly because most of them are left-handed, whereas most of us are right-handed. Or maybe it's because we lead horses from the left, saddle from the left, mount and dismount from the left, and, if we are right-handed, are heavier-handed with the right than we are with the left hand, causing the horse to be resistant on his right side. Whatever, I know that I usually have to work twice as much doing something to the right with a colt as I do to the left.

To pick up the right lead, walk with the fence on your left, and stay 2 or 3 feet away from it. You should be using a ring snaffle and have two hands on the reins.

First, take hold of the horse lightly with both reins. This restrains him slightly, and also elevates his front end a little.

Then use both reins to angle the horse's shoulders to the left, toward the fence. Use the right rein to keep his body straight and to prevent his head from cocking to the left. Apply your left leg just behind the cinch to drive his rear end slightly to the right, so his body is angled toward the fence.

Now, apply impulsion to make him break into the lope. Depending on how lazy or active he is, cluck to him, kick him on the left side of the belly, or swat him down the left hind leg with a rein. Always apply impulsion on the outside; that is, when you are moving to the right, apply it on the left side, and vice versa.

Angling the horse's body to the left, toward the fence, is similar to the position for two-tracking. This angle almost forces him to take the right lead. Maintaining light contact with the right rein "clears" his right shoulder, keeping it up and making it easy for him to "lead" with his inside (right) hind leg. Applying impulsion on the left side drives his rear end to the right, positioning him to lead with the right hind leg.

Most horses will naturally take the correct front lead when they lead with the hind leg first. That's why we concentrate

1/ Here are two pictures showing how I position the horse to pick up the correct lead without using a fence. I want the mare to pick up the right lead. I've collected her and am using my right leg to position her left shoulder to the left. This clears the right side so the right hind leg will initiate the lead departure.

2/ I have taken my right leg away and have added left leg to urge forward motion. I have kept contact with the reins and continue to hold the shoulders straight. She has started off in the right lead, level and comfortable.

1/ When a horse has difficulty departing on the correct lead, I'll use the fence as an aid. Here I'm trying to pick up the left lead. I had been traveling to the right, had stopped, backed a few steps, and now I'm rolling back into the fence.

2/ As I roll back, I have directed the mare to the left and added my right leg for impulsion. My left leg is away from her side so as not to confuse her. Her body is in good position because of the roll-back to take the left lead.

3/ *The mare has taken the left lead and I'm directing her in a left circle to build her confidence while traveling in this lead.*

Your cues should become imperceptible after much practice . . . and practice makes perfect.

on helping them pick up the correct lead behind.

To pick up the left lead, do everything just the opposite.

To summarize:

1/ Pick up lightly on both reins.

2/ Angle his shoulders toward the fence, but keep him basically straight and collected. It's difficult for him to pick up the lope if he's strung out.

3/ Move his rear end toward the inside with your outside leg.

4/ Apply impulsion.

If the horse takes the wrong lead, STOP. Reposition him and start again. If he continues to have problems, there are several reasons why:

1/ He is not maintaining the proper position when you request forward motion.

2/ He needs more work on leg control. That is, to get him to respond to your leg and move his hip over, and to be better at controlled forward motion.

3/ You need to work on controlling the horse's head, maintaining a flexible poll, rate of speed, and collection.

Gradually lessen the angle at which you turn the horse's shoulders until he will pick up the correct lead while keeping his body straight. Eventually, all you do is pick up the reins and get light contact, touch him with your outside leg, and he will immediately pick up the lope on the correct lead. Your cues should become imperceptible after much practice . . . and practice makes perfect.

11 CHANGING LEADS

"Dragging a lead" has cost many reiners a winning run.

TO SOME HORSEMEN, the flying change of leads is the biggest challenge in their reining program. Whereas they may have rock-solid confidence that their horses will slide and spin, they keep their fingers crossed that they will nail their changes.

It is probably also accurate to say that "dragging a lead" (changing the front lead but not the hind) has cost many reiners a winning run.

This is why reiners prefer what we describe as "deadly-leaded" horses, horses who will automatically change leads smoothly and precisely, with very little help whatsoever from their riders.

Why do reining exhibitors lack confidence in their ability to change leads? Possibly because it's human nature not to practice something we can't do well. Also, some riders probably do not practice lead changes because they lack an understanding of the components and the time necessary to develop them properly.

Practicing improperly can cause lack-of-control problems such as running through the bridle, charging when the horse feels your leg pressure, nervousness, high headedness, heavy mouth, and anticipation when coming across the middle of the arena.

You can't force a horse to change by simply spurring him or going faster and expect him to become a solid, dependable lead-changer. Take your time and *first* develop lead departures (picking up the correct lead), circles, leg control, poll control, and rate. Then when you position the horse correctly, he can easily make lead changes.

Teaching a horse to do a series of smooth, fluid changes is not difficult. If you build to it gradually, laying all the groundwork, it can be easier than you think. This is assuming, of course, that your horse has the athletic ability to do it, and you have the discipline and *feel* to teach it.

My goal is to change leads on a reining horse anywhere, any time. He should do it smoothly and quietly without moving his tail, speeding up, slowing down, bouncing the rider, or diving into his changes. He should change so fluidly that someone watching only the rider can't tell that the horse under him changed leads.

Finished Horse

Before explaining how I teach the change, it may help if I first explain how I ask a finished horse to change leads. Then you can better understand what I am trying to achieve. It makes no difference whether it's a reining horse, western riding horse, or horsemanship horse—I change them all the same.

Assume I am circling on the right lead, and I'm going to change to the left at a certain point. My horse is a good mover and is in a true, rhythmic, three-beat lope; he is not four-beating. Initially, I draw up on the reins slightly by moving my hand back a few inches to increase contact with the mouth and increase collection.

When I get contact, I do two things simultaneously:

1/ Move my rein hand slightly to the right to hold his shoulders in the circle to the right.

FINISHED HORSE

(A sequence of four.)

1/ *This sequence shows changing leads on a finished horse in the bridle. After galloping a circle to the left, I've collected her to initiate the lead change, and have her moving straight across the center of the arena. My right leg is against her side to straighten her body.*

2/ *I have checked back on the reins to raise her shoulders and have released my right leg.*

3/ She has changed leads, but I am keeping her on a straight line so she doesn't learn to duck off in the new direction.

4/ Now on the right lead, I've started to release the rein contact and allow her to level out and circle to the right.

2/ Put my left leg on him to move him over to the right for two or three strides. For those two or three strides, the horse is moving forward in a slight two-track to the right, with his right shoulder somewhat ahead of his rear end. This does what I call "clear the shoulder," in this case, the left shoulder.

By now I'm at the point where I want to ask the horse to change. Again, I do two things simultaneously:

1/ Check my hand back and to the right.

2/ Move my left leg away from the horse. When the leg pressure is released on his left side, his hip will follow my left leg, and when it does, he changes leads.

To change from the left lead to the right, I do everything just the opposite.

My method for changing leads has worked for many people who were having difficulty because of cueing the horse to change by spurring or applying pressure from the outside leg. My horses change when I *release* pressure from what becomes my *inside* leg. Although other methods work fine for many people, I feel that I can get smoother, prettier, and fancier changes with my method on most horses.

I do not neck-rein to cue the horse to change leads, although checking my hand back and away from the change is important in the early stages of training. Checking the reins back keeps the horse from speeding up or dropping his inside shoulder and diving into his change. When my horses are completely trained, they change leads, both front and behind simultaneously, off a very slight cue.

In teaching a horse to change leads when I release my leg pressure, I build to it gradually. It doesn't happen overnight.

I will set him up to change, then ask him to change by releasing what becomes my inside leg, and then immediately apply a bit of pressure from my outside leg to tell him what I want. Over a period of time, he learns to change when I simply release my inside leg.

On a finished horse, I never apply any outside leg pressure unless he misses the change or becomes lazy. For example, if he misses changing from the left to the right, I put my left leg on him, or maybe even boot him, and also check back on the reins to the left to keep him from speeding up or dropping his shoulder.

Sometimes, instead of adding more leg pressure, I'll cluck to my horse, using a verbal command to maintain forward motion.

I do not shift my body weight as a cue to change leads. I believe this throws the horse off balance, and possibly shifts more of his weight to his front end. That lets his hindquarters slide out of the circle, causing him to miss the hind-lead change. It's better to sit still and keep your weight in one place.

When my horses changes, I want his backbone straight because he can't change efficiently or smoothly if he has a bend in his body. I also want him to change leads in front and behind simultaneously. A front change first is mechanically wrong because that means the horse is dropping his shoulder. A hind change first is better, but changing both leads simultaneously is the correct way.

It's very important for the rider to feel what the horse is doing under him. Some people, no matter how many times they read this book, will not get their horses trained correctly unless they learn to feel what their mounts are doing.

When it comes to changing leads, I feel for an even cadence, and for the down

When my horse changes, I want his backbone straight because he can't change efficiently or smoothly if he has a bend in his body.

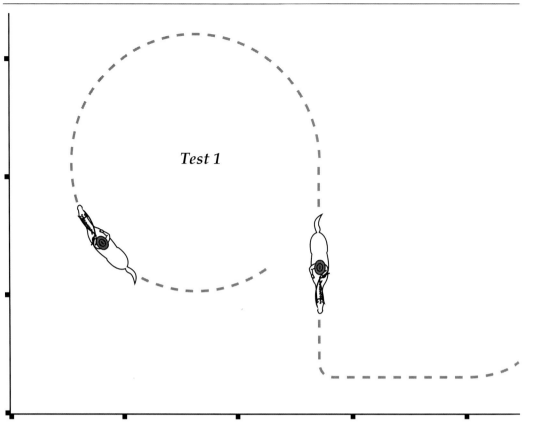

Test 1

When it comes to changing leads, I feel for an even cadence, and for the down stride of the front feet.

stride of the front feet. That is, I ask the horse to change when I feel his front feet going down and touching the ground. Then when they come up, he'll change. If I wait until his feet are coming up, they must come all the way up, go back down, and then come up and change.

Okay. That's how I ask a finished horse to change. Now let's talk about how we accomplish that.

Three Tests

After a colt can pick up his leads, has learned to two-track and side-pass, and is loping circles well, I want to find out if he has any talent for changing leads naturally. There are three tests I use to evaluate the colt, and I do them in the arena where I have a fence to help me.

In the first test, I lope big circles; assume I'm on the right lead. After a few circles, I straighten the colt out and aim him straight at the fence (see diagram No. 1). When we are five or six strides from the fence, his weight will start shifting from one side to the other because he doesn't know what to do. Sometimes he will change on his own. If he doesn't, as we are about to reach the fence I check back on my reins and add pressure from my right leg. If he's got any agility at all, he'll change leads, and I slowly direct him off to the left and go on. This tells me that the colt has a lot of natural ability.

When a colt fails to change leads, I can stop him into the fence. Then I can evaluate what occurred and work on the area of his resistance.

Usually, controlling the head or getting the colt more sensitive to leg pressure will prepare him for the next attempt.

The most difficult aspect of this drill is to keep him loping as we approach the fence, while not allowing his shoulder to drop. Therefore I do speed him up as we

Test 2

circle, then maintain the pace until after the change.

In another test (diagram No. 2), I gallop him diagonally across the arena and bring him into the fence at a 45-degree angle. When he's a couple of strides from the fence, I ask him to change. This angle sets him up in a good position to change, with a little help from me. If he changes easily, it tells me that he will probably be a pretty good lead-changer.

In a third test (diagram No. 3), the colt is almost forced to change leads. I bring him into the fence at about a 45-degree angle, and then almost roll him back to make him change. Sometimes this test will awaken a colt as to what he's supposed to do, and he'll go on to become a good lead-changer.

One thing I NEVER do in teaching a colt to change is drop to the trot to pick up the new lead. All that teaches him is to make what I call a lazy lead change and not to stay rounded and collected. If you always drop to the trot to change (called a simple change), pretty soon that's all the colt wants to do.

66 Drill

Now that I have a good idea of the colt's ability to change leads, we can go into all kinds of drills, and my favorite is what I call the 66 drill. Basically, it is an extension of test No. 2 we just discussed. Here's how you do it. At one end of the arena, make a circle, or several circles, with the colt under control and with you rating his speed. You should be moving at a controlled gallop.

After making several circles, head diagonally across the length of the arena to the

TEST NO. 2
(A sequence of three photos.)

1/ This sequence demonstrates one of the lead-changing tests (shown in diagram 2). After galloping a right-hand circle, I straighten my horse and head to the fence at about a 45-degree angle. Here, I have picked up both reins and applied my left rein against the neck to straighten up the left shoulder. I've also applied my left leg and, although it's not shown, I am keeping my right leg away from the horse's side, and very quiet.

2/ At this point I have started to initiate the lead change. I continue to hold my hands in basically the same position, but am checking them back toward my right hip. I have released my left leg and have applied my right leg lightly. Checking him back might slow his forward motion slightly. So now, depending on the horse, I may use a verbal cue like clucking, rather than using more leg pressure, to help maintain my original speed.

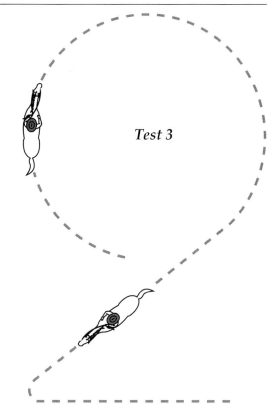

Test 3

3/ The palomino has changed from his right to his left lead and has stayed fairly straight during the process. The fence, which serves as a barrier to his forward motion, and my hand-check kept his body in the proper position for the lead change. If he doesn't change leads, or gets confused in any manner (speeding up, etc.), I'll stop at the fence, rollback to the right, and try again.

far end. Let's say you were circling on the left lead at the south end. Now head to the opposite corner, on the left lead, and at a relaxed gallop. When you are 25 or 30 feet from the fence, put your right leg against the colt to straighten his rib cage to the left. Maintain light contact on both reins to keep his head and neck straight and restrict his forward motion.

Aim for a spot on the fence about 20 feet from the corner. When you are about 10 feet from the fence (see diagram), remove your right leg and apply your left leg, if necessary, to move his hip under him. At the exact same time, check back slightly with both reins toward your left hip. He will change leads, and now you make several circles to the right at this end of the arena. Then repeat the drill in the opposite direction.

If he doesn't change leads, stop. Work a few minutes on making him move away from your leg pressure, in both directions. Then repeat the drill.

Be sure before attempting any of these drills that you have good control, collection, and can maintain a cadenced lope. Never let the horse break gait. Also, have proper leg control so you can keep the outside hip under the horse. Without these controls the colt may swing his hip to the

66 DRILL

This diagram illustrates what I call my 66 drill. Here's the sequence.

1/ I start by loping one or more circles at one end of the arena. In this diagram, I am loping circles on the left lead.

2/ I head diagonally across the arena on the left lead.

3/ When I am 25 or 30 feet from the fence, I put my right leg on the horse to move his rib cage to the left.

4/ When I am about 10 feet from the fence, I remove my right leg and apply my left leg, if necessary, to move his hip under him. At the exact same time, I check back slightly with both reins toward my left hip. He now changes leads.

5/ I make several circles to the right, then repeat the drill in the opposite direction.

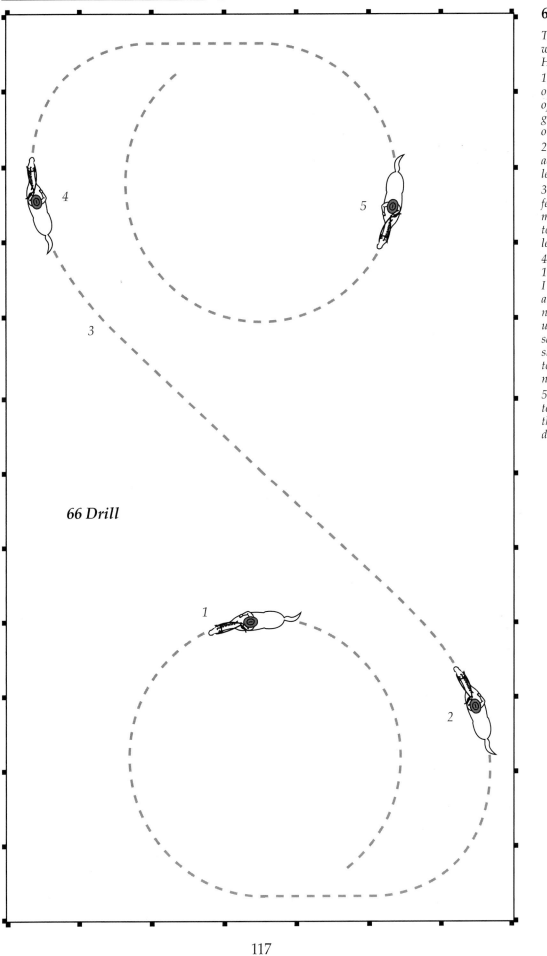

66 Drill

66 DRILL *(A sequence of four.)*

1/ This sequence demonstrates what I call the 66 drill. Here, I have been loping on the left lead diagonally across the arena, and am now approaching the corner. Approximately 4 strides from the fence, I further collect the horse and use my right leg to move his rib cage to the left. This frees up his right shoulder to change.

2/ When I change my legs, releasing pressure from my right and applying light pressure with my left, he changes leads and I continue going straight.

3/ After the change, I maintain my direction and control of the horse, not letting him speed up.

4/ At the fence, I turn smoothly to the right and continue on the right lead. If the horse had not changed leads, I would rollback to the left into the fence, stopping his forward motion as a reprimand, then try it again.

outside of the circle, making it difficult to stay in the correct lead or to change leads.

In the 66 drill, aiming the colt at a spot about 20 feet from the corner gives you adequate distance to turn, after the change, without ducking him off in the new direction. By this time, he's beginning to associate that when he approaches a fence, he's got to move his hip up under him and change leads—and that he changes when you check back on the reins and change legs on him.

The 66 drill also lays the groundwork for my eventual goal: that he changes when I move my leg away from him. After he's accomplished this drill, I'm ready to start changing him as we gallop across the center of the arena. When we reach the point where I want to change, I get contact with the horse's mouth, change my legs, and he should change leads on the straightaway.

Checking back on the reins is an integral part of this program. It not only keeps the horse from speeding up or dropping his shoulder, but takes the shoulder away from the change, allowing the hip to move to the inside. You do not steer the horse into the new direction until well after the change. Horses must be basically straight when they are asked to change. Some riders must also strongly resist the urge to rein a horse into the change, and learn to check back instead, clearing the shoulder.

Whenever a horse speeds up or charges through a change, I immediately stop him and back up. I might also bend him around to make him more hesitant about gaining forward motion. Then I put him back into a lope, and ask him to change again. Stopping him every time he gets chargey helps takes care of the problem, but I also continue to concentrate on poll control (keeping his face vertical) and rating his forward motion when I apply my leg.

Lead-Change Drill

When a colt is ready to perform a more formal lead change, I focus his training to solidify this maneuver by teaching him my lead-change drill. I usually teach a young horse this drill before I change leads too often.

Lead-Change Drill

In this drill, I make a nice round circle, or circles (1). Then I stop (2), side-pass into the circle (3), pick up the new lead (4), then continue loping straight ahead for several strides before moving into the new direction (5).

Let's assume I'm loping on the right lead. After I've loped a circle or even several circles, I come to a complete stop short of the center of the arena, and side-pass to the right about 6 feet. Then I hold his shoulders to the right and change my legs on the horse, loping off on the left lead, straight ahead. This forms the basis for everything I will do when I make the flying change of leads.

In other words, the horse should:

1/ Make a nice, round circle or circles.

2/ Have the ability to two-track slightly into the center of the circle. When his training is further along, you should keep him straight while loping across the center of the arena, with his shoulder away from the direction of the impending change. Straight is optimum.

3/ Then, when I hold his shoulder up by checking him back, and change my legs, he should change leads and continue

LEAD-CHANGE DRILL (*A sequence of eight.*)

1/ This sequence shows my lead-change drill. After loping a circle to the left, I head to the center of the arena.

2/ At the center, I stop.

3/ Then I add my right leg and side-pass to my left.

4/ I continue to side-pass until I feel the horse moving over willingly and freely.

120

5/ I change my legs and position the horse in a straight line.

6/ I ask the horse to take the right lead by clucking and applying left leg pressure.

7/ He starts forward with his right hind leg first. The rest of his body stays straight.

8/ Now on the right lead, he relaxes and waits for his next directive.

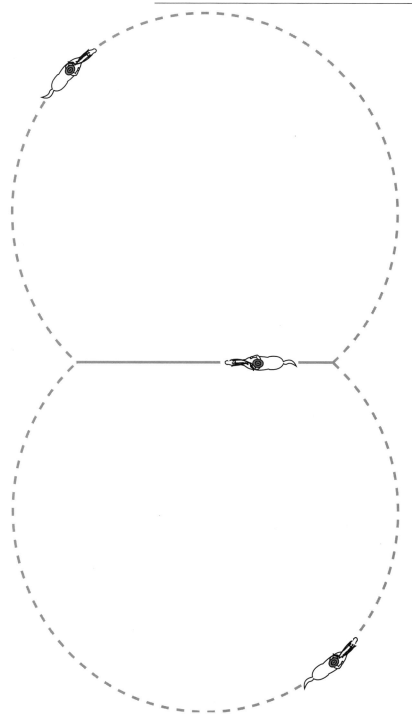

I like to make perfectly round circles, but when I'm going to change leads, I keep the horse on a straight line while coming across the middle of the arena.

apply the other, as necessary, just behind the front cinch.

For example, if I'm circling to the right and want to change to the left, I move my rein hand(s) back to the right, remove my left leg, and apply the right.

You may be wondering what this drill accomplishes that simply stopping and then picking up the other lead doesn't accomplish. When you stop and then pick up the new lead, the horse doesn't learn to respond to your leg pressure, or release of leg pressure. The same is true with the drop-to-the-trot change of leads. Besides, as I already mentioned, that teaches him to make a lazy lead change, and also causes his back to become concave rather than convex, which doesn't allow to him to become collected and change leads fluidly.

When the horse learns the lead-change drill, you can make him change leads at any place, any time by holding him over with your outside leg and then by checking him back slightly with the rein(s) while releasing your leg pressure. That's the beauty of this drill.

Also, since you are asking him to change by *releasing* your leg pressure, instead of booting or spurring him, his tail should stay quiet and he should stay more level.

This drill also teaches the horse to keep his body straight when he changes, and not to dive into his circles.

After doing this drill for maybe 2 weeks, the horse will become so accustomed to it that when you come to the center of the arena and check back on the reins, he will stop; as soon as you apply your outside leg, he will side-pass, and when you change legs, he will lope off in a straight line without dropping his hip or shoulder, and will move smoothly into the new circle.

Changing Without Stopping

Now we're ready for changing leads without stopping. I like to make two round circles, each about 100 feet or more in diameter. As the diagram shows, the two circles should connect in the center on a straight line.

I like to change leads on this straight line. Assume I'm loping on the right lead. As we

loping in a straight line.

When I check with my hand, that means I pull back slightly with my rein hand (or hands when I'm riding with a snaffle) in the opposite direction of the lead change. When I change legs, I remove one leg and

CHANGING WITHOUT STOPPING *(A sequence of eight.)*

1/ This sequence shows how I change leads on a young horse after he can perform my lead-change drill smoothly and easily. Here, I'm loping a left circle and have aimed toward the center of the arena.

2/ To prepare for the lead change, I've collected the gelding, and added my right leg to his side while keeping my left leg away.

3/ I'm two-tracking to the left while maintaining a cadenced lope.

4/ You can tell by his expression that the gelding is comfortable with the rein and leg pressure and is ready to change.

5/ *I've checked back lightly on the reins and have changed my legs, asking him to change. On a young horse, I do apply outside leg pressure to help him learn to change, but I do not on a finished horse unless he becomes lazy or misses the change.*

6/ *He willingly changes to the right lead and stays straight.*

7/ *I continue the cue for one full stride, and release my cues slowly. You don't give cues abruptly, or release them abruptly.*

8/ *Now, he continues loping straight with a good attitude, ready for whatever I ask him next.*

MORE ADVANCED HORSE

(A sequence of four.)

1/ When a horse is more advanced, I begin changing him without two-tracking him first. In this sequence, the palomino gelding changes from his right lead to the left. Here, we are coming straight across the middle of the arena. I have my left leg on him very lightly, and have him collected. He is straight and ready to change.

2/ I have released my left leg, applied light pressure with my right, and checked the reins back slightly.

125

3/ He makes a smooth change.

4/ Now traveling on the left lead, he continues loping without getting chargey, and with a pleasant expression.

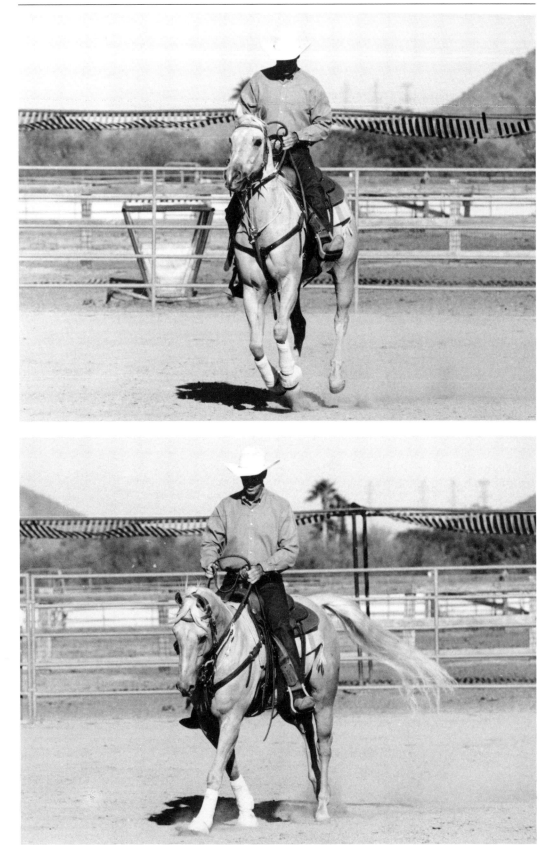

move onto the imaginary straight line, I apply my left leg and left rein and two-track to the right for about three strides. This "clears his left shoulder" so he does not lean toward the left, causing him to duck (drop) his shoulder to the left and miss changing his hind lead. Then to make the change, I simultaneously check my hands to the right, and release my left leg. If my horse is lazy or doesn't immediately change leads, I'll use my right leg to urge the hind legs to change.

The horse will change leads while staying in a straight line; then we move off into the other circle. I do not apply any rein pressure on the right side of his neck; that would cause his left shoulder to drop and also push him into the left circle; I want him to keep moving straight for several strides before turning into the new circle so he doesn't learn to duck off.

You can do all sorts of things in this lead-change drill. Normally, I two-track the horse about 2 feet into the center of the circle. But if he is anticipating the change, I might two-track him farther. Or I might drop my left leg off and continue in a right-hand circle. Or keep my left leg on him and change directions, but keep the horse on the right lead in a counter-canter. Or stop and back up. Or whatever is necessary to keep the horse fully controlled, and until he learns to keep his body straight while he changes.

If a horse begins anticipating, I will also lope complete circles on him in the incorrect lead and change leads while counter-cantering. In other words, change from the incorrect lead to the correct lead while maintaining the same circle.

As the horse progresses in this circle drill over a period of several months, he gradually learns to change when I check him back lightly with the reins, and simply move my outside leg away from him. I will no longer have to use my other leg. This is what results in smooth, pretty, precise changes.

COUNTER-CANTER

1/ The counter-canter can be utilized in many ways. For example, I can change leads out of the counter-canter to teach a horse the correct body position. Here, the horse is almost ready to change; all I would have to do is straighten him up with the reins, which would bring his inside (right) shoulder up, then change my legs.

2/ Counter-cantering on the right lead in a left circle to help teach the horse to keep his inside shoulder up. Counter-cantering can also help prevent a horse from anticipating the lead change. That is, when you come across the center, you change direction into the new circle, but do not change leads.

12 STOPS

Stops have improved not only in form and style, but also in the finesse used to achieve them.

THE LONG, DRAMATIC sliding stops performed by reining horses are one of the most exciting maneuvers seen in any horse show event. They not only thrill the crowd, but also the rider. It's an awesome feeling to be aboard a horse who gradually builds his speed with each stride until he's running rapidly, and then shuts down...burying his tail into the dirt while his front legs continue moving freely (reiners call it "pedaling").

Even though reining and stock horses in years past could make some impressive stops, stops today have improved consid-erably. You can't realize how much they have changed for the better until you look at old super 8 movie film of reiners taken in the 1960s and '70s, and even videos in the early 1980s.

Stops have not only improved in form and style, but also in the finesse used by the riders to achieve them. No longer are horses muscled to a stop. Today's top trainers and riders simply sit down in the saddle and say "whoa" while the finely tuned horse melts into the ground.

The momentum from his speed, and the power from his hindquarters, carry the

This mare is powering to a sliding stop in dramatic fashion as the result of running correctly and responding to the word whoa.

horse in a spectacular slide. All the while his front feet walk along, not jamming or propping, and his head stays in a natural position, with his mouth closed. Trailing behind is a set of perfectly aligned tracks, the "ll" so coveted by reiners. When the horse reaches the end of the slide, he gathers himself up and waits expectantly for the next signal from his rider.

That's how I would describe a perfect stop. It's smooth and spectacular, and to experience it on a good horse is like sitting astride a package of power-packed energy. It's an exhilarating experience when a horse bends his loins, driving his hocks low to the ground, and has the muscle and power to hold his position and slide while under full control.

How far you slide depends a great deal on the ground, but I'd say that 15 to 25 feet is excellent for most stops. Although I'm not opposed to longer stops, I do like a horse who wants to stop hard, bending his loin and laying his hocks close to the ground.

If the ground is hard or slick and you're running fast, you might go farther than you planned. The longest slide I've made was about 45 feet on hard, pebbly ground with a horse named Bar Thunder. The longest slide I ever made with Expensive Hobby was about 35 feet, but he was very deep in the ground.

The slide is so spectacular that most judges seem to put more emphasis on it than other parts of the pattern, even with today's scoring system. Obviously you must be able to circle, change leads, and turn around, but you could have a rough spot in one of those maneuvers and still win or place high if you make great stops. If the rest of your pattern is good and your stops are sensational, you'll probably go home with an award or a check.

On the other hand, if your stops are mediocre, you probably won't do well even if the rest of your pattern is outstanding. Judges give high marks to horses who stop big, and patterns have three or four stops versus two turn-arounds, two sets of circles, two lead changes, etc.

The real true-blue stopper can stop in any kind of ground—slick, hard, deep, or uneven. The horse who's built right and has been trained to break in the loins and drive his hocks under himself can stop in any ground. This horse is confident when he stops, and can handle different types of footing.

I'm confident of my horses' ability to stop and know I can ask them to get in the ground when it's deep, or when it's firmer, ask them to slide farther.

As I mentioned, a horse must be built right to stop this way. He's got to be stout through the loins, powerful in the hindquarters, and have good muscling in the gaskin, especially inside. With this kind of conformation, I can train a willing horse to stop the way I like.

The Basics

After I've been riding a colt about 90 days, I have him well under control, can rate his speed, and he has the general idea that "whoa" means stop. Now I want to find out if he can break in the loins and really get in the ground, and has what it takes to make quality stops.

I already have a pretty good idea if he can because of the way he backs up. The correct backing position is very much like the correct stopping position. To back, the horse must bend his back, shove his rear legs under him, and move in reverse gear fluidly and swiftly. If he can do that, he can probably stick his tail in the ground.

My cues to ask a colt to stop are similar to the way I ask a finished horse to stop. I sit down in the saddle, say whoa, then pick up the reins—in that sequence. The first two cues give the colt a chance to begin stopping before I take hold of him. As soon as he comes to a complete stop, I release the reins.

I believe you always have to give the horse "someplace to go" and reward him when he's doing well. Which is to say that if he does something correctly, he should get relief. If you put your leg on him to move him over and he moves, you remove your leg. If you pull on the bridle and he

The slide is so spectacular that most judges put more emphasis on it than other parts of the pattern.

129

DOUBLING FROM THE TROT

(A sequence of three.)

1/ Doubling can help a colt learn to stop. I first double a colt from a trot, staying fairly close to the fence.

2/ To double him, I sit down, loosen my outside rein, and pull toward my hip with the inside rein. I only pull as firmly as necessary to accomplish the turn.

stops, you release the reins. And so on. If you contain the horse and keep asking when he's already trying to do what you want, he will get confused.

Usually I start working on the stop while trotting big circles. I have more control of the colt at a trot than at a lope, and the fundamentals for stopping are the same. You could do it at a walk except that the colt won't have enough impulsion to get his hocks under him.

To stop from the trot, I sit down, say whoa, and pull back lightly. I pull one rein a bit more than the other to keep him flexible in front; pulling both reins equally tends to make a horse stiffen up and jam his front legs into the ground. I don't see-saw the reins, unless I get no response, because that can make his head go up. I simply take the slack out and use an offset pull.

As soon as he stops, I move my hands forward to relieve the bit pressure. I then let him stand quietly maybe 20 seconds, roll back, trot off, and ask him to stop again.

Most good colts will stop with just a light pull. With a colt who doesn't want to stop, or lacks the agility to stop, you must go through training processes to make stopping easier for him. I don't want to pull too hard. That would soon make him dread stopping and make him less responsive to the bit.

Doubling

I help a colt learn to stop by doubling him. In fact, I double all my colts because it improves their lateral flexibility. And I will double older horses who might need it. Doubling means turning a colt by bending his head and neck sharply. To begin this work, I double him into the fence.

I move out at a brisk trot, staying fairly close to the fence (assume it's on my right). When I'm ready, I reach down my right rein, sit down, say whoa, and then double the colt into the fence. I do this by

STOP, BACK, TURN *(A sequence of eight.)*

1/ This is another exercise that can help a colt learn to stop correctly. From the trot, I stop and then back the colt until he is backing freely.

2/ Then I will pull my inside rein while the colt is still backing. This makes him lift his front end and shift his weight to his hindquarters.

3/ I continue a light pull through the 180-degree turn, then trot off in the opposite direction.

4/ I trot on a loose rein, but go only a short distance before repeating the exercise.

5/ *I have stopped and am backing the colt straight, alongside the fence.*

6/ *When he's backing freely, I pull on the left rein toward my hip until he has turned 180 degrees.*

7/ *After doing this a few times, the colt is more relaxed and supple.*

8/ *This time when I ask him to stop, he is trying harder to use himself in a collected manner. After several more backs and turns, I should be able to lighten my pull because he will understand the signal better. Then his front end will begin softening instead of being so stiff. As I progress, the colt will stay more flexible in front while stopping.*

You can improve the stop by working on the back-up.

loosening my outside (left) rein and pulling the right rein toward my hip. I pull him all the way through the turn so we are facing the opposite direction. Without hesitating, I break him off into the trot again, travel about 75 or 100 feet, then repeat the drill, this time doubling him to the left. To get impulsion in the turn, I use my outside leg behind the front cinch.

Doubling accomplishes several things:

1/ Since it stops his forward motion, he learns to begin stopping when he hears the verbal signal *whoa*.

2/ It makes him learn to use his loins and to drive his hindquarters under him.

3/ He learns to get his inside hock under him when I pull on the inside rein. If I'm going to double him to the right and pull on the right rein, he drives his right hock under him so that leg can be the pivot point.

4/ It keeps his front end flexible. Instead of jamming his front feet into the ground, he learns to use them to help push himself around.

Suppose you have a colt who is stiff or awkward. When you try to double him, his shoulders keep going straight ahead even though you have his head pulled toward the fence. You should apply more pressure on the outside. If you're trying to double him to the right, either drive him with your left leg or smack him down his left rear leg with a bridle rein. This will drive him into the fence, making him a believer that he has to follow his nose in the direction it's being pulled.

After a colt has been doubled into the fence a few times each way, he will start slowing or thinking *stop* on his own when I say whoa.

I continue this for a few more days, then I'm going to fool him. I trot down the fence (assume it's on my right), sit down, and say whoa. He expects to be doubled to the right, so he plants his right rear leg under him. But I out-fox him by pulling the left rein a little more than the right. That makes him bring his left rear leg under him also . . . so both hind legs are under him, and I've got a pretty nice stop. If he has completed it well, I let him stand a few moments and pat him on the neck.

Then I try it again. From where he's standing, I back him a few steps, then turn into the fence and break him off into a trot. When he's relaxed and moving fluidly (not anticipating), again I sit down and say whoa. Thinking that he's going to be doubled to the left, he brings the left hind leg under him; but I pull more on the right rein, bringing that leg under him, too. Again, he should make a nice stop. I let him stand, pat him, then trot off and do something else for a while.

If your horse still isn't paying attention to the bridle after this drill, or he's not getting his hocks under him like he should, forget asking him to stop and work on improving his back-up. As I mentioned at the beginning of this chapter, the stopping position is almost the same as the backing position, and you can improve the stop by working on the back-up.

When you pick up the reins to ask the horse to stop or back up, his body should fold like an accordion. His head should give to the bridle, and his rear end should come to his head. Refer to the chapter on backing. Try to improve your horse's agility and flexibility so he can flow backwards.

A horse who backs stiffly will never be able to "glide into the ground" because he will be stiff and rigid. We want him to be able to gallop at full speed, then just melt into the ground. Depending on the particular horse, you may have to work on backing him for several weeks, but it's well worth the time and the best way to improve his stopping ability.

With the good colt who quickly learns to stop well when he's doubled from the trot, I begin asking him to stop from the lope. I use the same procedure, and will even double him into the fence from the lope.

When it becomes firmly fixed in the colt's mind that he folds into the ground

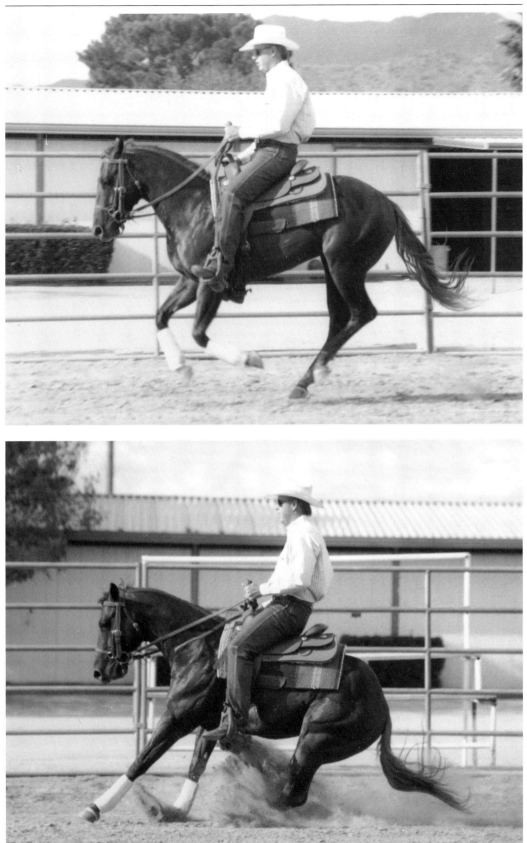

STOPPING & BACKING

(A sequence of five.)

1/ *When I'm stopping a young horse who's not solid (he's a little stiff, pulls on me a little bit, and is not confident in his stops) I hold him and balance him before and during the stop. Here, I've collected this colt and have his head in a position where I've got control; that is, he can't get his head away from me very easily.*

2/ *I sit down and say whoa and hold my hands steady. I might use a give-and-take pull on the reins to keep his head in position. An uneven pull makes it harder for him to resist the pull.*

3/ He is starting to flex at the poll and has rounded his back, driving his hind legs forward to balance himself in the stop.

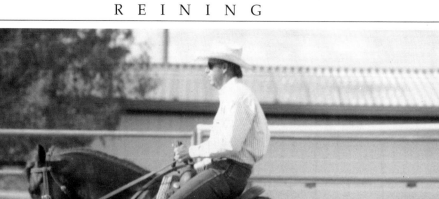

4/ Although the colt did stop very well, he needs to improve the beginning of his stops. Therefore after he stopped, I backed him up while repeatedly saying whoa. This will make him more responsive and lighter on the bit.

5/ *A few minutes later, I ask the colt to stop again, and this time he responds by really getting on his hocks, deep in the ground. Notice that I have released some rein pressure to allow him to slide.*

when I give him the three cues, I begin increasing the length of his stops by speeding up. More speed gives more momentum for sliding farther. At this stage, I use the same three cues: sit down, say whoa, and pull back lightly. I do not pull hard just because we are going faster. No matter how fast a horse may be galloping, you stop him with finesse, not strength.

Adding Another Cue

By now, I've probably been riding the colt approximately 6 months. If he's a good colt, he's stopping well from the gallop. Now I will add a preliminary signal to my sequence of cues. Before I say whoa, I move my rein hand forward a couple of inches, for just one or two strides. Next, I will sit down and say whoa simultaneously, then take the slack out of the reins. Here's the reasoning for releasing the bridle reins for a split second:

When a reining horse is galloping correctly, he is, in effect, running uphill. His head stays in the correct position, his front end is elevated, and his hindquarters are

driving. If you ask him to stop when he's running like this—when he's in midair with his legs fully extended—he will go into the ground too abruptly. He can't slide like he should, and he'll probably bounce a time or two.

You must allow the horse to level out his front end and shorten his stride just a hair. I accomplish that by moving my rein hand forward and releasing the curb chain or bit pressure. Then when I sit down and say whoa, it's much easier for the horse to get into what we call a "soft start." That means he just melts into the ground.

On a finished reining horse, as soon as I drop him off the bridle, he levels out and

Sometimes you have to analyze in what part of the stop a problem is occurring.

starts getting his hindquarters under him. As I sit down and say whoa, he begins stopping before I ever pick up on the reins.

On a horse who's burning down the arena, this sequence of cues happens so fast they become almost simultaneous. From the time I move my hand forward until the horse begins stopping, he has probably taken only one or two strides. As he is stopping, I sit as steadily as I possibly can—keeping my legs quiet and my seat in the saddle. And I keep just enough pressure on the reins to hold the horse in the stop.

One thing I should clarify is the term "sit down in the saddle" when I ask the horse to stop. This doesn't mean I've been standing in the stirrups beforehand. Instead, it refers to a redistribution of my weight. When I'm galloping a reining horse, I am sitting down—but only about 60 percent of my weight is in the seat of the saddle. The other 40 percent is in my stirrups. When I ask the horse to stop, I round my back slightly and roll my hips under me so about 90% of my weight is now in the seat of the saddle.

I think it's very important to stay as quiet and as balanced as you can. It's tough for a horse to stop correctly if your weight is shifting around on his back.

Problems

Let's say this horse is stopping pretty well, but then he develops a problem. For example, suppose I am moving at a brisk lope when I drop off the bridle just a hair, sit down and say whoa, then start to gently pull. The horse gets into the ground a little bit, but doesn't stop completely. What to do?

I'll probably double him. While loping I ask him to stop and then immediately take one rein and pull his front end around so he has to drive his inside back leg under him. As soon as he comes around, I set him down to stop his forward motion, then back him up. What this does is accentuate my request for him to stop; he knows that he will be reprimanded if he doesn't.

The next time I lope him down the arena and say whoa, he's going to be thinking harder about how to get into the stop. But if he doesn't stop, I double him the other way, which will "even up his sides." Generally this is all that's necessary to get a good horse stopping correctly again.

Sometimes you have to analyze in what part of the stop a problem is occurring . . . the beginning, the middle, or maybe the horse is walking out of it at the end. If it's at the beginning, you might need to pull the horse a little harder or quicker initially, then ease up on the bridle reins and let him go ahead and glide.

If he's walking out of the stop at the end, then you need to take a little more hold of him toward the end of his slide to keep him in the ground . . . even to the point of him thinking "back-up" at the end of his stops.

If he's not getting any distance to his slides, the solution is to add speed, keep him relaxed, and keep his hocks pushing evenly. Leave his head as loose as you can so that he can slide and stay relaxed. Then he'll walk along in front instead of jamming his front feet into the ground and stopping abruptly. If you overpull, you're going to get him too deep in the ground, and then he won't get any distance at all.

Sometimes I must vary from my sequence of cues in stopping a horse. Take, for example, a horse who is low-necked, or who runs downhill. I continue to drive him and lift the reins to elevate his front end all the way through the run. When I reach the point of the stop, I merely sit down and say whoa, and continue to keep light tension on the reins. This keeps him balanced properly so he can get his rear end under him to sit down and slide.

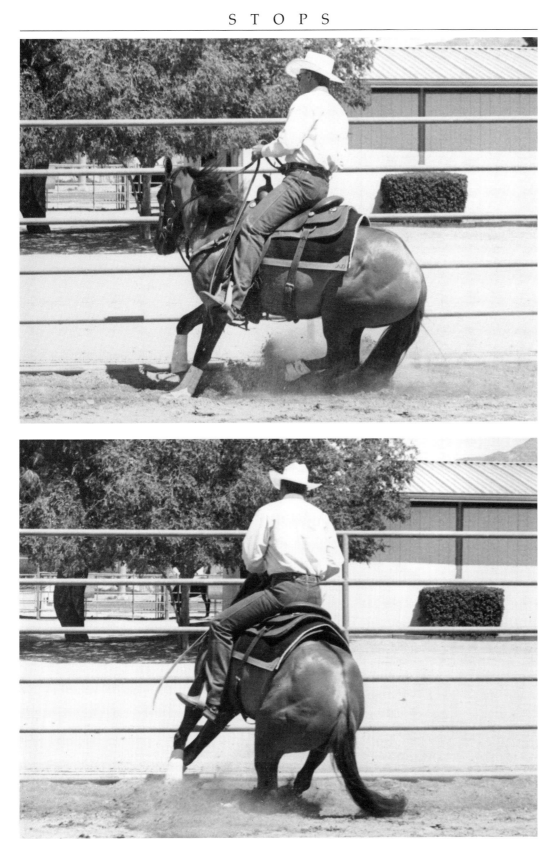

DOUBLING FROM THE LOPE

(A sequence of four.)

1/ *Doubling a horse into the fence can improve a horse's stop because it forces him to shift his energy to his hindquarters to balance himself. It also gets him on his hocks quicker when you say whoa. From the lope, I say whoa and immediately turn him into the fence.*

2/ *The horse should respond quickly and get on his hocks. Because I am pulling with only one rein, his body stays supple during the stop and turn. As this horse starts to turn, he lowers his head so it doesn't interfere with the fence.*

3/ *After he completes the turn, I let him gallop off, then collect him again, say whoa, and repeat the exercise.*

4/ *After a few turns on the fence, the horse should be more responsive to the word whoa. Here, even though I'm using very little pull, my horse quickly melts into the ground for a balanced stop.*

DOUBLING, NOT USING FENCE

(A sequence of five.)

1/ This is another good sequence showing what can be achieved when a horse is doubled. Here, I have sat down and taken the slack out of my left rein. I am going to double this gelding several times to improve his hock drive. Notice that because of my pull on the left rein, the left hock is driving harder.

2/ I continue to pull with only my left rein all the way through the turn. If he were to resist, I would continue pulling him around to the left (in one or more full turns) to achieve the desired response. After he completes the 180-degree turn, I break him into a gallop.

3/ As I sit down and pick up the right rein, he drives his right hock deep into the ground. If I had pulled too quick or too hard, it would have made his rear end come out of the ground and swing to the left.

4/ Notice that I have slack in my left rein, allowing the palomino to bend in the direction he is being pulled. This picture shows how I pull to my hip, and how the horse bends or doubles through the turn using his inside (right) pivot foot.

5/ Now the gelding is willing and ready to stop. Notice how he is bending in the loins, and how he's driving his left hock under him since I'm picking up more on the left rein than the right. If I were to pick up both reins, both hind legs would drive well up under him in a comfortable, relaxed stop.

As you and your horse get the hang of stopping, you will develop a feel for how much you need to pull him. Most of the time, the horse will tell you how much to pull. This means that after you have released the bridle as the first cue, then picked up the reins again and are holding the reins steady, the horse will take hold of the bit to balance himself while he slides.

NEVER overpower the horse to stop him. If you go flying down the arena and then rip his head off, he'll start scotching badly in his run-downs, or will dive into his stops to brace himself and protect his mouth.

This brings us to the subject of bits. I'm a devout believer that if you cannot get a horse to stop in the snaffle, you're probably not going to get him to stop well in anything. If you have to use force to make him stop, he will never be as solid as you want him to be.

To be a great stopper, a horse must want to stop. That's why a reining horse must have a super mind and a willing attitude.

Pulling

Throughout this chapter, I have talked about pulling on the horse. Using the term *pulling* may give the impression that I am strong-arming the horse, using force, but this is not true. I pull with only enough pressure to accomplish what I am trying to do. For a horse to have a light, responsive mouth he must be taught to respond properly to pressure. If the horse is light and responsive, a very light pull is all that's necessary. And it gets even lighter as the horse responds more quickly.

With a tougher, less responsive horse, I have to pull a little harder or use more bridle until he understands what I want. Then I can start using lighter pulls. The goal with any horse is to see how lightly you can cue him to achieve the desired response.

**RUN-DOWN
TO STOP**

(A sequence of five.)

*1/ Now I am schooling
this palomino gelding in a
run-down to a stop. As I
increase his speed, I keep
him flexed and collected.*

Bits

Once a horse stops well in the snaffle, you've got to find a bit he is comfortable with when you show him. Horses vary in their preferences; some like a bit with more weight, or a higher port, or a lower port, or more leverage.

Sometimes when we put more bridle (a bit with more leverage) on a horse, he can balance himself better in the stop. Or the opposite can be true. Sometimes we have too much bridle on a horse and we need to back off. A case in point is the horse who wants to raise his head too much in the stop. We shouldn't put more bridle on him to "hold his nose down"; we should try to relax him by using a milder bit on him, if possible.

You may have to go through a number of bits before you find one the horse likes best. That's why most trainers have a variety of bits hanging in their tack rooms.

Whether I use a curb chain or curb strap depends on the horse. If he's light-mouthed and responsive, there's nothing nicer to show him in than a flat leather curb strap because you get a nice feel of the horse without roughing the chin groove. When a horse is exceptionally light and I want to balance him on the bridle (bit), I use a curb strap because a chain might back him off the bridle too much (scare him).

But I'm not adverse to using a curb chain. I'm not out to impress anybody by riding with a curb strap. If a curb chain will increase the lightness and responsiveness of a horse without scaring him, I'll use it. When a horse is not responding well to a mild bit and leather curb, I think it's better to put more bridle and a curb chain on him rather than pulling harder.

The Run-Down

The run-down deserves attention because, in my opinion, the stop is an extension of the run, and the run is all-important in how well the horse stops. If the horse isn't running correctly, he can't stop correctly.

144

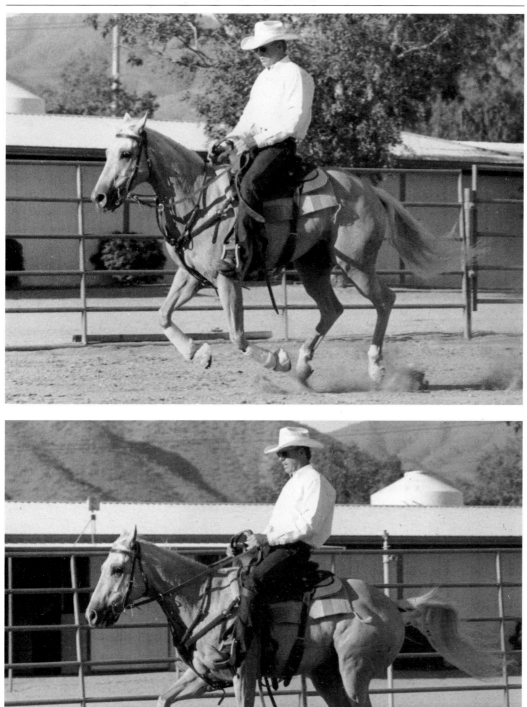

2/ I am concentrating on sitting quietly, straight, and behind the motion as we approach the stop. The horse remains collected and relaxed.

3/ When I feel the front feet come down, I sit down and say whoa. I keep my hands in the same position, and hold them steady to balance the horse. I do not pull abruptly.

4/ The gelding melts into the ground with his shoulders elevated, his front legs relaxed, and his head in a good position.

5/ As I feel him break in the loins and drive his hind legs forward, I loosen the reins to reward him and let him slide.

STOPPING IN THE BRIDLE

(A sequence of four.)

1/ This mare is running uphill to the stop. I have released my contact, thereby releasing the curb-chain pressure as my first signal to stop. Notice that the mare is out of the bridle somewhat (beyond the vertical). Her head should stay vertical, even when I release my contact.

2/ As I sit and say whoa, she drops into the ground to slide. Her front end is slightly braced at this point, so I try not to pull because that would cause her to brace even more.

3/ I sit quietly and wait, allowing her to adjust and feel comfortable while stopping. Her front end is supple as she bends in the loins and gets deeper into the ground behind.

4/ She glides along in the slide in an eye-pleasing, balanced manner. Before I ask her to stop again, I need to get her more flexible so she will stay relaxed in the poll, neck, and front legs. That will improve her approach and initiation of the stop.

On my track I have short fences at either end that I use for "fencing" my horses. This young horse is learning to use himself well as he has progressed in this exercise.

During the run-down, you need full control of the horse so you can rate his speed, and he must run in a straight line. I start this with a colt by trotting him from one end of the arena to the other—all the way into the fence. (Reiners call it "fencing the horse.") If he begins to drift off, say to the right, I bring him back on course with the left rein. Later when he's farther along in his training, he will know to stay between the reins. If he drifts, I can straighten him up with a neck-rein.

When the colt has trotted all the way to the fence, I sit down and say whoa, but don't pull. I let him stop by himself while I concentrate on keeping him straight. I don't want him to develop the habit of veering off. I want him to go straight into the fence. When he will trot nicely down the arena in a straight line, I begin loping him.

I keep him at a slow lope. Again, my primary goal is teaching him to lope down the arena collected and in a straight line. Obviously, if a horse is drifting or leaning from one side to the other when he's running, he can't stop as straight or get the distance in his slide that he can when he's running straight.

When he's a few strides from the fence, I sit down and say whoa, and let him stop by himself.

The next step is to teach him to rate his speed. I always start slowly, and with a green horse, I might even let him trot a few strides before breaking into a lope. Then each stride he takes should be a little bit faster so he reaches the desired speed before the end of his run. You want the horse running uphill into his stop. You cannot get a fabulous stop from a horse running downhill since his weight is more on his front end than his hindquarters.

We don't want the horse to break into a dead run immediately because then he has no way to build speed. And you should NEVER start the horse slowly and keep him slow through most of his run-down, then ask for a sudden burst of speed just before asking him to stop. That will result in the horse learning to back off when you ask for speed . . . leveling out too soon or scotching.

149

FENCING IN ARENA

(A sequence of four.)

1/ *In this sequence I am fencing a bridle horse in my arena. I have gained speed until I reached my desired stopping speed. I'm riding behind the motion, concentrating on maintaining my horse's speed as we approach the fence. I don't want him to slow down and start dropping his shoulders because then he would stop on his front end.*

2/ *As my horse starts into the ground, he stays straight, not ducking off to his right or left. He is beginning to stop because we are approaching the fence, not because I have signaled him.*

3/ He is in a terrific position as he slides toward the fence. I am sitting quietly, as I do whenever I stop.

4/ He finishes his stop just before reaching the fence. Fencing helps any horse learn to stop, and also prevents him from anticipating the stop in a shorter run. He learns that he must run all the way to the fence.

The culmination of proper training is an awesome stop! This is Matt Kimes' good gelding Flash Me A Chic.

He should start his run with a lot of control, and each stride should be a little bit faster until you attain the maximum speed *you* want. I say that because there are some horses you don't want to run wide open—those who can't control their stop as well as they can when they are rated back just a little.

When you reach that optimum desired speed, that's when you should stop. The horse will be slightly elevated and running uphill into the stop, and his momentum will carry him forward into a slide. If he were slowing down, it would be more difficult for him to get his hindquarters under him.

Fencing a Finished Horse

Every time I head toward a stop, whether in the practice pen or show ring, I want the horse to think he's going all the way to the fence. I don't want him to think he's stopping when he's 40 feet from the fence. If he starts checking, he will not have the kind of motion going into the ground that he needs to make a beautiful stop. Therefore, I will occasionally fence a finished horse, galloping him right to the fence.

However, I am careful about how I do this because I'm an advocate of a horse wanting to run to the fence. He certainly won't if he's punished and driven into the fence too hard, time after time. Here's how I do it:

About 20 feet from the fence, I drop some slack into the bridle reins, say whoa, and steer him only to keep him straight. I let him go into the fence anyway he wants to. In other words, I don't ask him to stop; I let him do it on his own.

That makes him get his hindquarters under him, which saves some work on my part. Plus I think most horses enjoy it. But they won't if they are driven into the fence harder and harder. Eventually, it will be difficult to get him anywhere close to the fence.

It also reveals that the horse might not be willing to run. If the rider does this time after time, the horse will get smarter and smarter. He knows that when the rider guns him, the stop is next, and the horse may decide to skip the speed and stop before being asked.

While the horse is running, I keep light contact with the reins to rate his speed. He needs the bridle for balance, and I need to keep light contact so I can rate his speed, and keep his head in a good position as he runs.

Once a horse understands that he runs from "fence to fence," you don't have to do it very often. In fact, you shouldn't. If you need to work on stops, you can do it without fencing him. You can lope around the arena (staying off the rail), build speed gradually, and then while he's on the straightaway, ask him to stop, as you must do in many reining patterns. Even when you are running around the end of the arena, the horse should think *run* all the way, and never anticipate stopping.

Some of the reining horse trainers have oval tracks in their pastures or fields, with the footing carefully prepared to facilitate sliding. These tracks have no perimeter fencing—only short fences at each end for fencing.

You can usually teach a horse to rate his speed in a field or on a track better than you can in the arena. Once again . . . in the arena, the horse is thinking "barn," or "gate," or is distracted by other horses. Out in a wide open area, there are no distractions. I can let a horse run for maybe 300 feet, then pick him up and lope for another 300 feet, then gain speed again. Once you have the control to rate a horse in the open, it's a great advantage when you take him in the arena.

In the patterns requiring that you run around the end of the arena, rather than up and down the center, you can school the horse in the same manner. It is even more important that you can rate your speed properly to keep the horse from wanting to run, with less control, around the ends of the arena.

You should build your horse's speed in the same manner—and be able to hold the desired stopping speed for several strides. I like to practice running long, and when I show I never want to stop until I am a good distance past the designated markers.

Once a horse knows how to stop, and can stop well, I don't do it very often. It simply isn't necessary when a horse is broke; continuing to do it will take some of the sparkle and style out of his stop.

These are good ways of keeping full control of a horse's speed and mind. I don't want him to learn to take charge, anticipate, or get sour.

When I was showing Expensive Hobby in reining and cowhorse classes, rarely did I ever stop him hard except in a class. I knew him so well, and had so much faith in him, that I knew he'd stop the best he could whenever I asked him.

153

13 TURN-AROUNDS

Overall, the horse should give the impression of flowing around with extreme speed.

LIKE OTHER maneuvers in the reining pattern, I start this one slowly, building my foundation. Initially, I ask only for half-turns, but my goal is for a colt to plant his pivot foot and turn around smoothly, with consistency. Although speed is essential in a turn-around, you've got to have form first.

The turn-around should be flat, with no up-and-down motion or hopping. That's wasted motion. The horse should plant his inside hind foot as his pivot foot, and practically drill a hole into the ground with it while he turns. The outside hind foot is the driver; it helps push the horse around, as does the outside front leg. The inside front leg comes off the ground, moves over, and sets down out of the way of the outside leg, which crosses over it. Overall, the horse should give an impression of flowing around with extreme speed. That's the way I like a horse to turn around.

This is vividly shown in the videotapes of many top reining horses, such as winners of the National Reining Horse Association aged events. The turn-arounds of those horses are spectacular to watch, and if you analyze the motion of those horses,

Turn-arounds are thrilling to spectators and exhilarating to the rider when a horse turns with finesse and dynamic speed. This horse is turning low to the ground, staying on his correct pivot foot, and has good reach with his front legs. The latter enables him to turn with a lot of speed.

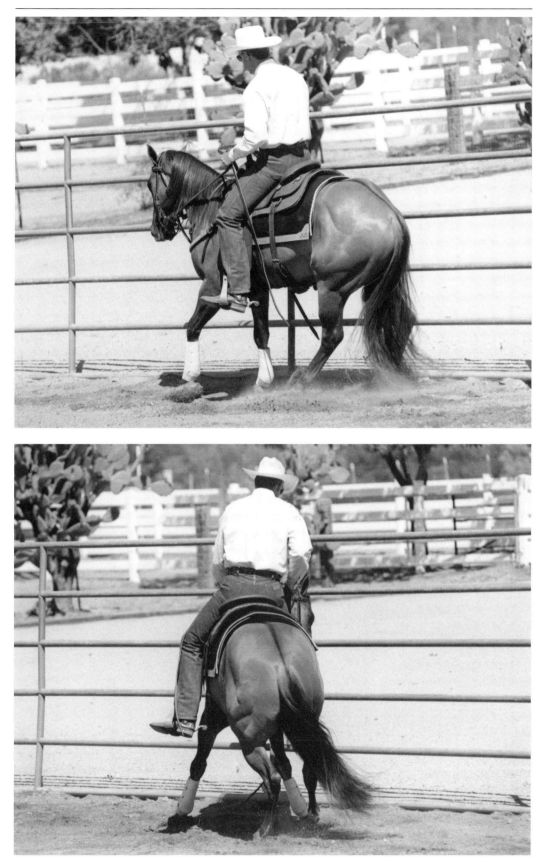

FENCE DRILL
(A sequence of five.)

1/ After I have the fundamentals on a colt, I start developing his turns by using this simple drill. Here, I have positioned my horse next to the fence and have begun backing.

2/ When my colt is backing freely with some dispatch, I loosen my outside rein and continue pulling lightly with my inside, or fence-side, rein.

155

3/ *The momentum of the back-up is carrying him through the turn. The fence acts as a barrier, teaching the colt to sweep around with his front end.*

4/ *I release my reins after the colt turns 180 degrees.*

5/ Then I go back to "neutral," and walk quietly, before repeating this drill in the opposite direction. Walking a short distance keeps the colt calm and relaxed.

you can see that they are not trotting or loping around. I don't know of any term for how those horses are turning, other than *fast* and *flat*.

In addition to turning with form and speed, a horse must also be under precise control so he can shut down instantly. In other words, if a reining pattern calls for four turn-arounds, you must stop exactly where you started, after completing four revolutions. Over- or under-spinning results in penalty points.

I'm ready to start teaching the turn-around when a colt will follow his nose when I pull the inside rein. He knows how to walk, trot, and lope a circle with his neck, shoulders, rib cage, and rear end all following his nose on the same track. I've rolled him into the fence, and when this happens, he knows to bring his inside hock under him. With just a very light pull on the bridle, he backs up straight with some dispatch.

I want to emphasize that the colt must be able to walk and trot in a small circle and follow his nose, giving to the rein correctly, like he does when circling a bush. The colt should be able to make smaller and smaller circles, keeping his body in line but flexible.

By this time, a lot of good colts have so much feel and ability that it's a great temptation to make a full turn (360 degrees). But you've got to restrain yourself. First grade must always be completed before second grade, and the colt must learn to make a good half-turn first.

Let's assume I'm going to make a half-turn to the right. I gather the colt up and begin backing him, lightly and quickly alongside the fence, which is on

BACK & HALF-TURN DRILL

(A sequence of five.)

1/ After the colt has become proficient at making half-turns on the fence, I work on half-turns without using the fence. This keeps the colt from anticipating the direction of the turn. This young horse is backing quickly and calmly.

2/ At this point, I release my right rein and continue lightly pulling my left. The colt begins arcing for a left turn.

3/ He has set his pivot foot (left hind) and has begun elevating his front end to turn. I am pulling straight back to my left hip to ensure the colt making a half-turn onto his same tracks.

4/ Because of the momentum from backing, the colt sets his hindquarters and sweeps his front end around.

5/ The colt is just finishing the 180-degree turn. I will now stop and release the reins, allowing him to relax.

I like this method because backing puts the colt on his rear end, and isolates the rear end while the front end turns itself.

my right. When I'm ready to turn, I simply drop pressure off the left rein while I keep contact with the right; I do not pull any harder. This allows his head to come around to the right a little, into the fence. Since he knows how to follow his head, that, combined with the motion from backing up, automatically results in his body flowing around and over his hocks in a half-turn.

That is the foundation of my turn-around. At this point, I apply very little pressure with my outside rein, but I might apply pressure from my outside leg to make his side follow through. A lot of extra impulsion should not be necessary because the colt has plenty of motion if he is backing properly. I simply redirect that motion with my inside rein to turn the colt over his hocks into the fence.

I like this method because backing puts the colt on his rear end, and isolates the rear end while the front end turns itself. If the colt were simply standing still, or even walking in a small circle, I would have to pull too hard to get him to turn and also isolate the hind end at the same time. Backing the colt sets him on his rear end, and dropping the outside rein lets him flow over himself without my pulling on him, or driving him with my leg for impulsion. It's a very simple method. It teaches him to plant his pivot foot and turn freely.

A good colt who is agile and well schooled in the basics can make this half-turn easily. After he can do it well in both directions, the next step is to turn him with a little forward motion. I'll trot him forward in a medium-size circle, then do what I call *set him*. I check back on the reins to stop his forward movement, release pressure on the outside rein, and pull lightly with the inside rein to bring him around in a half-turn. I pause to let him think about what we've done, then ask him the to do same in the opposite direction.

With the ideal colt, I am still asking him to turn by only pulling lightly on the inside rein (and, of course, I'm riding with a snaffle). Checking or setting him with the outside rein puts him on his hocks, and pulling on the inside rein redirects his forward motion into a half-turn. Doing this while moving in a circle makes it easier on the colt because it gives him direction.

The colt is ready for the next step when he can:

1/ Make these half-turns fluidly and easily with only a light pull on the inside rein.

2/ Walk and trot in very small circles following his nose, without his hip escaping to the outside.

3/ Back quickly from a very light pull, with his head in the vertical frame.

4/ Stay flexed at the poll when bending laterally.

The next step is to take the colt through some very small turns, walking slowly and easily. Earlier, I said I didn't want to make a full turn from a circle because the colt didn't know how to plant his rear end yet. But now he does because of all the backing and half-turn exercises.

CURLY Q's *(A sequence of six.)*

1/ After this 2-year-old is making half-turns well, he's ready to advance to what we call curly q's—a full-turn exercise. I start by walking in a relaxed manner.

2/ I reach down my right rein, preparing to make a right turn. I draw up on the reins and collect the colt. When he's almost stopped, I begin the turn.

3/ He will set his pivot foot and follow his nose into the turn.

4/ While applying light outside leg pressure, I continue to direct the colt around in the turn. At this stage, I'm working on form, not speed.

5/ I finish the 360-degree turn. This was the first time I had asked this colt to make a full turn, and he did well.

6/ I loosen my reins to reward him, and walk off again. After he is relaxed, I will again ask for a full turn, using the same method.

While I'm walking him in a small circle, I check him back lightly to get him on his rear end, and ask him to turn around. I primarily use the inside rein (directing his head), but I might use the outside rein for a little stimulus to bring his shoulder. He will eventually turn from the outside rein only.

While he's slowly turning, I can watch over his inside shoulder to make sure his inside front foot is getting out of the way, and that the outside front foot is crossing over properly.

When he does this well in both directions, it's time to add some forward impulsion so he turns with more speed. I'll pull a little bit more on the inside rein to make his shoulders come around faster. And I will use a little outside rein on the neck and outside foot on the ribs to generate more speed, and to make sure the outside of his body is following well.

If a colt comprehends most of what I have taught him so far, but lacks agility, I take him to a corner in the arena and trot several faster, small circles. I concentrate on increasing his forward motion and getting him to trot around in rhythmic fashion with his shoulders up straight—not leaning like a motorcycle in a hard turn. Once he can do that, I use light contact to screw him down into a flatter, more forward-type of turn-around. (Having the fence on two sides helps contain him.) This gets him to thinking *forward* and *around*. This should help make it easier for him to flow around and cross his front legs over, rather than shifting his weight backwards onto the outside rear leg.

Here's something that may help you better comprehend a turn-around. While using a snaffle bit, you point the horse's nose, still keeping his poll flexed, and the body tries to catch up. The faster the nose goes, the faster the body and legs must come. When you finally put the horse in the bridle (curb bit) and touch him with the outside rein, his nose should still lead slightly while his body and legs try to catch up.

We drill this into him through repetition while he's still in the snaffle. We show him the proper form with repetition. Gradually I use less inside rein and more outside rein to ask him to turn; he knows that his head should always turn first (while flexed at the poll), followed by his neck, shoulders, and side. He should go faster and faster, depending on how much touch you have on the outside of his neck, or his response to your outside leg impulsion.

The really good, responsive horses have so much feel on their necks that when you touch them with the outside rein, they react as if it is scalding hot. Then it takes very little rein pressure to achieve the proper response.

You have to be careful not to use too much outside rein too soon. That can cause the head to arc to the outside if the horse hasn't been trained properly to this point and can't follow his nose. If you *always* have his head leading into the turn during his early training, he will always position his head that way. That makes it easier to position his head correctly when he advances to the bridle and you ride with one hand.

To ask for more speed, use a verbal cue (clucking) or use your outside foot as the accelerator, generally right in the area between the front and back cinches. That drives the rib cage toward your inside hand, with which you're lightly pulling. If the horse is broke properly and knows to follow his nose, the more you push with your outside foot, the faster he should go. However, do not just hang your foot in the belly. This will aid in desensitizing the sides, as well as make the horse want to reverse his arc and look to the outside. Instead, tap-tap-tap with your outside foot.

You have to be careful not to use too much outside rein too soon.

163

CIRCLE DRILL
(A sequence of six.)

1/ *I like this circle drill because it can do several things at the same time, all of which help the colt learn to turn around properly. It will lighten the mouth, keep the shoulders mobile, and help teach the colt to use his rear end properly. In this picture, I have completed walking and trotting several circles approximately eight to ten feet in diameter. My horse circled well, following his nose with his shoulders and hindquarters on the perimeter of the circle. Now I have stopped.*

2/ *The horse has been in a slight right arc while circling. I maintain the right arc and make a half-turn, staying on the perimeter of the circle.*

3/ I continue to maintain the right arc as I back around the perimeter of the circle.

4/ This drill increases the horse's flexibility at the poll, both laterally and vertically, as you can see here. This enhances my control when making full turns.

5/ *After backing around in a full circle, the colt feels light and is backing freely.*

6/ *At this point, I turn to the right by releasing some left-rein pressure. I allow the colt to make a full turn or more, still maintaining the right arc.*

If he's dragging his outside shoulder, you can encourage it to move faster by using your foot at the elbow or shoulder. But again, use caution. Make sure you have checked him back a little to get his rear end under him. Otherwise, if you go to the shoulder without giving him good direction (meaning he's not following his nose properly), it will cause his rear end to come out of the ground, and he will do what we call "swap ends." Then, both his front end and back end turn, instead of his hindquarters staying planted in the ground.

If you have followed all these steps carefully and have a talented horse, he will keep his hindquarters planted, move his front end well, follow his nose, and bring the outside of his body correctly. You can go as fast as you want, for as many turns as you want, depending on how much impulsion you use.

Problems

Thus far we have assumed we are working with a good colt . . . one who has no trouble making half-turns and can easily make full turns. But we are not always fortunate enough to have such agile colts, so let's go back and look at some of the problems we can encounter, in making either half-turns, full turns, or both.

Here are several that are typical:

1/ The colt lacks agility in his front end, and interferes in front, stepping on himself.

2/ He rocks too far back over his hocks.

3/ He doesn't stay on his pivot foot.

4/ He wants to use his outside hind foot as his pivot foot.

5/ He lacks impulsion when he comes around.

Here again, the rider must be skilled enough to tell what the problem is, which is why it's so important to be able to feel what the horse is doing under you. You must be able to tell if his outside shoulder is dragging, or his rib cage is hanging out, or whatever.

Problem 1—Lacks agility, and interferes in front. First, stand in front of the colt and take a good look at his front end, especially the width of his chest. Maybe he's simply too wide, and it's physically impossible for him to turn correctly. Also look at his front legs. If he's extremely toed-out, that can prevent him from turning properly. And ask yourself if the colt is really agile. You should be able to tell by how well he backs, gives his head, circles, and half-turns.

If the colt is too wide through the chest, has bad front legs, or is really stiff and lacks coordination, you might have to aim him at another event that requires less athletic talent. But if you think he still shows promise for reining, trotting a lot of circles, as we have already explained, will increase his agility for turning around. Sometimes if a horse is a little crooked, corrective shoeing can help him turn around cleaner.

Keep the colt's body in the proper position. Gradually make the circles smaller so the colt learns to cross his outside front foot over the inside . . . as he must do in a turn-around. Continue decreasing the size of the circles until he anchors his rear end and crosses his outside front leg over the inside leg as he turns. Then move him out and begin trotting larger circles again. We often refer to these circles as curly q's. One set of the accompanying photographs shows a colt making curly q's at the walk.

You can also double this colt on the fence, and back him and make half-turns until he learns to use his front end correctly. When you ask him for the half-turn, applying outside impulsion will drive him around the inside rein. I like to do this with a colt by holding my inside rein on my leg and pulling back on my outside rein until he turns. Then, I'll release the outside neck-rein to let him walk out of the turn. I'll repeat the turn again by simply picking up on the outside rein.

I can also slow this colt down to a walking turn-around, making him step all the way across his inside front foot with the outside foot. I can watch his feet by looking over his inside shoulder. This will teach him that he can turn without interfering. I will do this slowly time and time again. I will not ask him to move any faster until he knows how to handle his

The rider must be skilled enough to tell what the problem is.

167

CORNER DRILL— A YOUNG HORSE
(A sequence of six.)

1/ *I use a corner of the arena to help a young horse perform a turn-around. Having a fence on two sides as a barrier makes it easier for the horse to go around with forward motion. I first walk and trot several circles in the corner. I won't allow this filly to actually turn around until her circles are fluid and truly round. She is following her nose in a right turn.*

2/ *I use leg pressure to drive her forward, into the corner. The fences direct her around to the right, helping her front end to turn.*

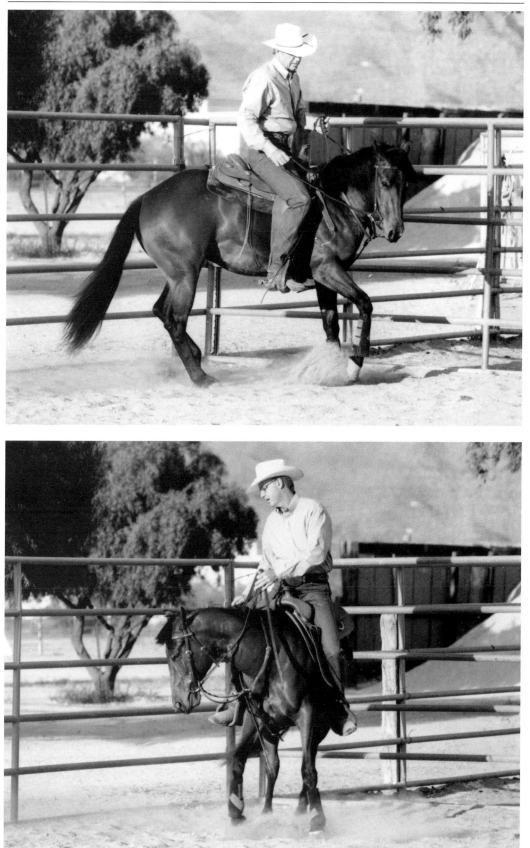

3/ As she drives off the fence, I use my reins to direct her around to the fence again.

4/ Her momentum carries her through the turn and back toward the fence with only slight encouragement from me.

5/ The process is repeated again as the filly crosses over with her front legs because of her forward motion.

6/ After she screws down for a couple of turns, I let her trot out in the circle again.

front feet and has the confidence that he can turn without hurting himself.

This is a good time to mention that it's always smart to use splint and bell boots on a horse who interferes. Then the horse will not hurt himself if he bangs one foot against the opposite leg or foot. That will not only discourage him from turning, it can also cause injuries that put him out of action.

Problem 2—Rocks too far back over his hocks. The solution is to add more forward motion to his turn-around, and one way is to trot a lot of circles, as explained under Problem 1. Some trainers also like to lope circles the same way . . . making them progressively smaller until the horse is turning in place.

Something else you can do is add impulsion on the outside. Go to his belly with your outside leg, and hold both reins with slightly more pressure on the inside, keeping the poll flexed. This will push him forward and make him drive to the bridle and step up. You can also make half- or full-turns, and drive him out of the turns with your outside leg. In other words, after making just a half-turn or one full turn, immediately break him out of the turn into a fast trot, in a straight line. Doing this several times will begin to make him think "forward" when he's turning; not rocking back.

Be careful to not put too much tension against the neck with the reins when turning him, as that will prevent him from moving freely with forward motion. The added rein pressure can slow his turn by making him reverse his arc, or can pull him back, putting him on the outside (wrong) foot to pivot. That will also slow his speed.

Problem 3—Doesn't plant his pivot foot. That's easy for me to fix since I'm big on backing a colt. I would back him and make half-turns until he learns to handle his front end with his inside hind foot stationary, or isolated.

Problem 4—Wants to use his outside hind foot as his pivot foot. In order to turn around correctly, a colt must learn to use his *inside* hind foot as his pivot foot. Some colts like to use their outside foot. When this happens, several things occur. First, a colt cannot turn with as much speed because he tends to suck back on his hindquarters.

Second, instead of crossing over with his outside front foot, he crosses under because he can't get his inside foot out of the way fast enough. That causes him to hop around, instead of staying flat. Third, the front legs tend to interfere more, resulting in splints and other injuries.

I have found that if I work a horse consistently for 30 days, I can get him over this problem. I start by having him make a quarter-turn correctly, then walk off. I repeat this time and again until the horse does it correctly on his own. Then I progress to making a half-turn correctly, walk him off, stop, and repeat. When he makes a half-turn correctly, I progress to a slow full-turn.

Eventually he will automatically use his inside foot as the pivot foot and turn with more forward motion, instead of rocking back.

I have found that, in some cases, it's better not to use spurs when working on this problem. That can make a horse cranky and cause him to switch his tail. Instead, for forward impulsion, I'll whack him down the outside hind leg with the ends of my bridle reins.

Problem 5—Lacks impulsion. When a colt is lazy or just not listening, he needs to be motivated to come around faster, and I'll usually cluck, then swat him with a rein down the outside rear leg. You don't have to worry about losing the hindquarters when you do this, because anytime you whack a horse on the rear end, his hind legs are going to come up under him. Plus as long as you whack him on the outside rear leg, you will keep him on his pivot foot. And it's going to motivate him to move, NOW! Soon he will associate clucking to motivation. Clucking then will be all the stimulus you need.

CORNER DRILL— A MORE ADVANCED HORSE

(A sequence of seven.)

1/ After a young horse is turning around well, the corner drill can help him learn to turn faster while maintaining correct positioning. While trotting circles in the corner, the horse's natural inclination is to come out of the corner, heading away from the fence. That's what this colt was trying to do here, bowing his rib cage to his right.

2/ Using my right leg, I drove the colt back into the corner. On this revolution, I will use my right rein and right leg to make him follow his nose in the turn instead of drifting out.

3/ I have started my drive through the turn again and back to the fence. When the horse's nose is close to the fence, I release my right leg and rein pressure for a split second to reward him, before continuing the turn.

4/ Once the horse wants to stay in the corner without drifting out, I add outside rein to screw him down into a spin.

5/ His speed has increased because his outside ribs and shoulder are following his nose better. He is driving the outside of his body forward toward his head. When this colt's turns improve, I'll straighten him up rather than keep him in a bent position.

6/ Maintaining good position and speed, the horse continues to turn willingly. I continue to direct him with the reins, and am clucking for impulsion.

174

7/ After a few good turns, I allow him to straighten out. From here, I will go to the next corner to make turns in the opposite direction.

Spurring

If clucking and swatting the colt down the hind leg doesn't work, a knowledgeable rider could boot or spur the colt in the belly, or even in the shoulder. I say "knowledgeable" because he has to be savvy enough to know which method would be best for the particular colt. I personally like to leave the shoulder alone as much as possible because if you harass it too much, you sometimes lose the rear end—it will jump out of the ground.

This is not to say I'll never poke a horse with a spur, because most horses, at one time or another, need to be spurred. There is a time and place for it, if you know how to use spurs correctly. Sometimes you need something a little sharper than a nudge of your heel to correct the horse when part of his body is out of position, or when he doesn't respond to your leg, such as when you are in the show ring and need an instantaneous reaction. Once a horse is trained, it's okay to use an outside spur for impulsion because by this time he should have his form correct and he will stay on his pivot foot.

I wear my spurs most of the time while I'm riding. The few occasions I take them off are on horses who don't respond well to spurs . . . a light spur doesn't get the desired reaction, and a hard spur gets a radical reaction. With this kind of horse, it's often better to boot him hard in the belly with your heel. He will turn better, with less resistance, than he would with a spur. It's of the utmost importance to keep a horse trying hard but maintaining a good attitude.

1/

2/

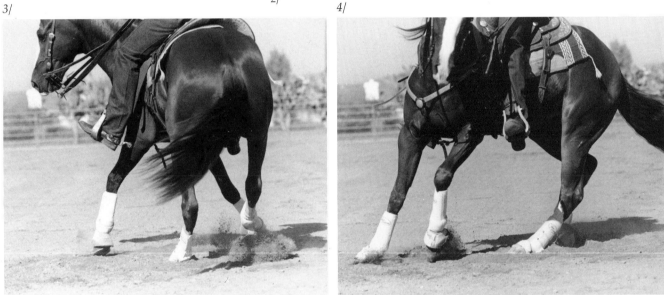

3/

4/

LEG ACTION (*A sequence of seven.*)
This sequence depicts an advanced horse in the bridle who is ready to show. I've asked him to turn to the left, and he has responded quickly and accurately. Note how well he is crossing over in front, and keeping his pivot foot planted. Because he has a lot of reach with his front legs, he can turn with added impulsion. In the last picture, I have completed the turn and stopped right where I started.

If you don't know how to use spurs, you won't get the optimum out of your horse, and you will also have a tendency to spur him when you shouldn't. So it would be best to leave them off.

Whenever I do spur or spank a horse, I always follow this rule of thumb: Be sure when you add impulsion that you give direction with your rein. Otherwise the horse doesn't grasp the significance of

5/

6/

7/

To make a fancy turn-around, you've got to have forward motion, you've got to have the horse on his inside pivot foot, and you've got to have the entire outside of his body moving. If the horse isn't giving the outside of his body, he can't continue to drive around his pivot foot. So if his ribs are out, or his shoulder, or head, or even his hips, you're not going to get the full speed and flatness you want.

why you are spurring, and you may get an undesired reaction.

For example, suppose I'm asking for more speed in a turn-around to the right. If I reach up and spur him in the left shoulder, I use my inside rein to direct that motion to the right. If I didn't, he might turn his head around and look to the left; it's typical for a horse to look back to the side on which he's spurred.

177

SCHOOLING AN OLDER HORSE

When schooling an older horse to sharpen his turns, I sometimes use the snaffle. I can pull with a snaffle to get the correct form and not scare or hurt him as you could with a curb bit. In the top picture, I have started a turn and am gaining speed. I have pointed his nose into the turn because he was not bringing his front end around quickly enough. I gave a quick bump on my left rein and at the same time applied my right spur to his outside rib cage. This added form and impulsion quickens his turn. Below, he is turning fluidly.

Other Problems

There are also other situations you may encounter with your horse. Possibly he's dragging his outside shoulder, or his rib cage is hanging out. This is why it's so important that you are sitting with your seat screwed down in the saddle; then you can feel what the horse is doing, and identify these situations.

If the outside shoulder is dragging, sometimes all that's necessary to correct this is impulsion from the outside rein . . . or maybe a tap on the elbow with your stirrup.

If his rib cage is hanging out, his rear end may fishtail out from under him. The correction: Drive the belly with your outside leg. By "hanging out," I mean that the rib cage is not aligned with the neck, shoulder, and hip. It's sticking out to the left, if the horse is turning to the right, and vice-versa.

To make a fancy turn-around, you've got to have forward motion, you've got to have the horse on his inside pivot foot, and you've got to have the entire outside of his body moving. If the horse isn't giving the outside of his body, he can't continue to drive around his pivot foot. So if his ribs are out, or his shoulder, or head, or even his hips, you're not going to get the full speed and flatness you want.

Speaking of the head, when the horse is turning, I want his head slightly to the inside so I can see his inside eye. This brings up another important reason why I always train colts in a snaffle. Because of the way the snaffle works and the positioning of its rings on the side of the head, the snaffle brings the entire head and neck when the horse turns. A bosal—or any similar gear on the nose—pulls the chin but "leaves the ear;" that is, the head is tilted with the chin to the inside and the ear to the outside. You certainly don't want that.

Clucking

We haven't said very much about clucking to the horse, as a form of impulsion in the turn-around. Many trainers do it, and so do I, but not to all of my horses. I definitely do not cluck to a horse who tends to be hyper because it would only make him more hyper. I want to keep him quiet.

On the other hand, I will cluck to a slower horse, but he needs to relate the cluck to immediately being poked in the belly, or smacked down the hindleg if he doesn't respond. Then when I cluck to him in the show ring, it means something—to speed up.

A final note on turn-arounds. When I teach the colt to do a 360-degree turn, and when he does it well and feels comfortable doing it, I like to turn him a couple of times, say whoa, drop my reins, then just let him stand a few minutes. This enhances the relaxation of the horse, and lets him think about what he's done.

I also like to do this after a horse has made a good, long, hard stop. I'll let him stand so he can gather his wits, relax, and settle. It lets him know he did it correctly, and it's also a form of reward.

One thing we haven't discussed in this chapter is how to turn a finished horse in the show ring, but we do have several photographs of a finished horse turning, and we also cover the subject in chapter 16, "Running a Pattern."

If his rib cage is hanging out, his rear end may fishtail out from under him.

179

FINISHED HORSE

(A sequence of three.)

1/ *With a finished horse I'm showing, I walk quietly to the center of the arena, if the pattern calls for turn-arounds first. I stop and stand quietly. My hand is low, by his neck, but when I pick up the reins, it should be like plugging him in. For a right turn, I move my hand slightly to the right. At the same time, I'm rocking my legs (in and out, next to his sides) to alert him, and to ask for forward motion. But before he takes a complete step forward, he will begin turning to the right because of my hand direction.*

2/ *I stay in rhythm with the horse as he turns, and cluck for speed.*

3/ *If I need to, I'll bump him with my left (outside) leg to urge him on. He will turn until I say whoa and release all cues.*

14 ROLLBACKS

A rollback is a snappy 180-degree turn over the hocks, executed when the horse's forward motion ceases after a stop.

ROLLBACKS are a very important part of today's reining patterns, and much emphasis is put on how a horse performs them. A smooth, quick rollback after an average sliding stop might result in a "plus" from the judge.

By definition, a rollback is a snappy 180-degree turn over the hocks, executed when the horse's forward motion ceases after a stop. Immediately upon completing the turn, the horse moves out in the same tracks he made approaching the stop.

Rules for reining stipulate that the horse must immediately break into a lope when

coming out of a rollback. Trotting out of a rollback results in a penalty.

Our colt already has the foundation for a rollback since he knows how to stop, back, and turn around. I have also rolled him back as part of his training for other maneuvers.

When I specifically begin working on his rollbacks, I am still riding him in the snaffle. I lope him alongside the arena fence, say whoa, and let him come to a complete stop. I back him up several steps, then make a 180-degree turn, and lope out of it. When I ask him to turn, this is the

STARTING THE ROLLBACK

(A sequence of five.)

1/ When I begin working a colt on rollbacks, I lope him alongside the arena fence, say whoa, and stop. Then I begin backing him up, as I'm doing here.

182

2/ I back him several steps.

3/ Then I ask him to turn 180 degrees.

183

4/ I primarily use a direct rein, when I'm using a snaffle bit, then some neck-rein and a little bit of outside leg.

5/ As he completes the turn I break him into a lope.

sequence of what I do:

1/ I primarily use a direct rein to point him into the turn.

2/ I add some neck-rein to turn his shoulders.

3/ I add a little bit of outside leg to make the hip follow and to help him pick up the correct lead.

I follow this procedure several times until the colt learns to turn 180 degrees without his front feet touching the ground, and immediately lope out on the correct lead. I no longer back him up first because it is only part of the training for rollbacks. When showing, if you back up more than two strides before rolling back, you get a score of zero.

When the colt's ready to make a more finished rollback, I let him come to a complete stop; then, with only a slight hesitation, begin the rollback. In the roll-back, there's a little trick I use. In fact, I use it on almost all my horses to prevent them from turning around too far. I rein the horse through the first half of the roll-back (90 degrees), then I release the rein pressure, but add my outside leg to com-plete the 180. This results in a smooth, flowing turn, with the horse moving out right in his tracks.

Reining him through the entire 180-degree turn would add too much momen-tum to the turn, and he will turn too far. For example, if you are rolling back to the left, he will end up to the left of the tracks he made coming in. This will make it difficult for him to depart in the correct lead (left).

I learned that if I rein the horse through the first 90 degrees, or quarter-turn, and then follow up with my outside leg, we end up right on our tracks. To me, that's very important.

When I'm judging, I penalize horses who make a U-turn, rather than rolling straight back over their hocks.

When we come out of the rollback, I don't want him to break and run wide open; I want full control. If I have done my homework, I've taught this colt how to rate by speeding him up and slowing him down, time after time. I have also con-centrated on making smooth lead depar-tures. Now when we gallop out after rolling back, I can pick up my rein hand and rate him to the speed I want.

If you have trouble getting your horse to roll back correctly, analyze what he is doing. If he's not keeping his rear end planted, stop him straight, back a few steps, and roll him off. This teaches him where his rear end should be.

If he's dragging his outside shoulder, use more neck-rein, or bump him in the outside elbow with your stirrup. Or if he doesn't roll back with any snap, swat him down the outside rear leg to add impulsion.

Correct timing on the rider's part also helps the horse perform this maneuver correctly. If the rider asks the horse to roll back before he has completed his stop, he will flounder around trying to do it.

In the rollback, there's a little trick I use.

ROLLING BACK, FROM A LOPE *(A sequence of four.)*

1/ As a young horse progresses, I do not ask him to back up first. Here, I have asked him to stop from a lope.

2/ After he completes the stop, I hesitate for a split second, then immediately ask him to roll back into the fence.

3/ When he's halfway through the rollback, I release the rein pressure and add pressure from my outside leg.

4/ Pressure from my outside leg helps him to move out, right in the same tracks he made going into the rollback. Reining all the way through the rollback usually causes the horse to turn too far.

ROLLING BACK, NO FENCE (*A sequence of three.*)
1/ Once the horse understands the fundamentals, I can ask him to roll back without using a fence. He's gone to the ground nicely as he stops.

2/ I initiate the rollback with my inside (right) rein and follow it with some neck-rein, and light pressure from my outside leg.

3/ In the ideal rollback, the colt sweeps around. At this point, I'm applying more pressure from my outside leg and have released the rein pressure. When a young horse can roll back this well in a snaffle, away from the fence, it's an easy transition for him to roll back in a bridle.

When we come out of the rollback, I don't want him to break and run wide open; I want full control. If I have done my homework, I've taught this colt how to rate by speeding him up and slowing him down, time after time.

15 ADVANCING TO THE BRIDLE

THE IDEAL in training a bridle horse is to take him from the snaffle into the hackamore, and from the hackamore into the

This shows where I like the bosal to be positioned on the nose. I like the hackamore to affect the bridge of the nose rather than the soft area below the bridge.

bridle. You can skip the hackamore, but if I have my choice, I'll go to the hackamore after the snaffle.

I feel that the longer you keep a horse in the hackamore, the better. The best reining horses I've ever ridden have been in the hackamore for almost a full year prior to going into the bridle. I developed their skills in the hackamore equally as well as I did in the snaffle, putting a good, solid foundation on them.

I'm not talking about a mechanical hackamore that has shanks and a curb chain and works on leverage. I am referring to a rawhide or leather braided bosal with a rawhide core, used with the traditional mane hair mecate (reins).

When a colt is ready, I ride him in the snaffle and hackamore simultaneously for several weeks; I put the hackamore under the snaffle. Since I have good control of the horse in the snaffle, I use it to ease him into the hackamore. I don't want to rough him up with the hackamore (bosal) when teaching him to accept it.

I'm very careful when I ride a colt in the hackamore, and like to use a little heavier, looser-fitting bosal. The added weight gives it more feel to the colt, helping him learn how to respond to it. The looser fit makes it drop off the chin readily when I release the pressure, again helping the colt learn how to work in it. If it didn't drop off, he wouldn't learn that the give-and-take is for response and relief (reward).

Once the colt knows how to respond correctly, I find a bosal that he's comfortable with and works the best in. Some horses like a bosal that fits fairly snug around the nose; others like a looser fit. Sensitive horses will get along better in a softer, lighter bosal of braided latigo, rather than a heavier bosal of braided rawhide.

On the majority of my horses, I use a little looser kind of bosal so that when I take hold of it, it works more on the nose than on the jawbones. This is necessary for the proper response. Yet I'm very careful not to rough up the nose because it's so important. Without a good nose, you won't have a good hackamore horse. Sometimes I'll even wrap the nose of the bosal with a material like latex to keep the nose soft.

I don't worry that much about the jaws. Although I don't like to sore them, what's really important is to have a good nose so the horse responds and gives his head easily in the hackamore.

If you work on the jaws, usually the horse's head will stay in a more natural position, or even be up a little bit. When you work on the nose, he'll usually drop

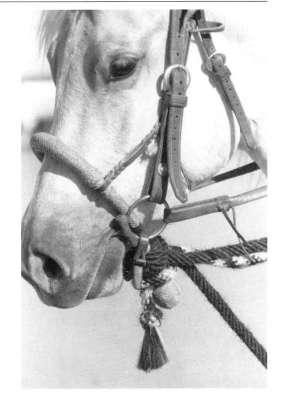

When a colt is ready to move into the hackamore, I'll ride him in both a snaffle and hackamore for a few weeks.

Photo by Kurt Markus

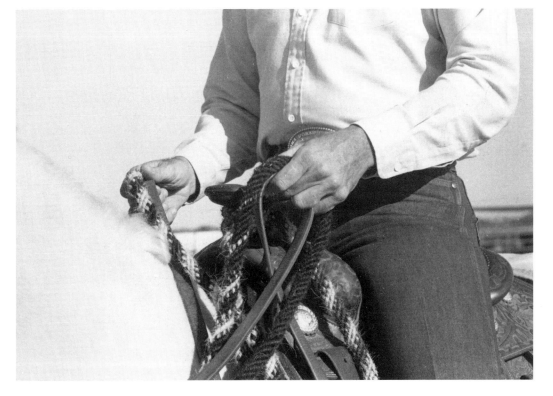

Here's how I hold the reins when the horse is in both the snaffle and hackamore. I hold both left reins in my left hand, and right reins in my right hand. This simultaneous pull gradually teaches the horse how to respond correctly to the hackamore.

Photo by Kurt Markus

189

After the horse graduates to only the hackamore, here's how I hold the mecate reins.

My hands are in a relaxed position, and the horse's head is responding correctly to the hackamore.

When backing, the horse should flex at the poll, just as he should in a snaffle.

his head down into the hackamore a little more, flexing at the poll. You have to do both to keep proper control of the horse.

When I'm riding a colt with both a snaffle and hackamore, I hold the left reins in my left hand, and the right reins in my right. I use the hackamore and snaffle reins simultaneously until the horse finally relates to the hackamore as well as he does the snaffle. Then I stop using the snaffle, and ride with just the hackamore, schooling the horse in all the maneuvers he's already learned until he does them equally well in the hackamore.

There are precautions to take. When you turn the horse in a hackamore, you are pulling on the lower part of his jaw rather than his mouth. But you still want the entire head, ears, neck, and body to follow, just like you do in the snaffle. Make sure the "whole horse" is coming when you pull on the hackamore, so you get the same correct movement as you did in the snaffle.

Also remember that a hackamore is not made to tug on. If you use a straight pull,

When using a hackamore, you want the head, ears, poll, neck, and entire body to follow the pull, just as you do with a snaffle. This horse is bending properly in a flexing exercise.

191

These two pictures show the horse correctly following the pull of the hackamore in a slow turn-around. As I speed the turn up, the horse will become straighter.

The horse continues to hold the correct form as he picks up speed in a turn-around to the right.

often the horse can push his nose right through the hackamore and maybe get away from you. You'll get much better results with the hackamore by using a give-and-take motion with your hand. Then the horse will have less tendency to take hold of the hackamore and bull through it.

But regardless of what you use on the horse—snaffle, hackamore, curb bit—if you abuse him with it to the point he gets mad, he can take his head away from you. The horse has incredible strength in his head and neck and there's no way you can outmuscle him.

We have to use common sense and know that whenever we do take hold of the horse, we should have the advantage. In other words, you should have him pointed in a certain direction so that if he gets confused, or tries to take his head away from you, he will go where you have him pointed—such as in a circle where it's easier for you to regain control.

When it's possible, I like to keep a horse in the hackamore at least one full year. Then I move him into what we call two reins—using a light bridle and the hackamore simultaneously. I usually use a small, pencil-type bosal under the bridle.

The bit I use depends on the horse. Is he heavy-headed or light? But generally I use a bit that's fairly thick in the bars of the mouthpiece because the horse can feel this bit better and take a little more hold because it's a lot milder than a bit with thin bars. I sometimes use a leather chin strap instead of a chain curb.

I want to give this horse every chance to be light in the bridle. Some horses who are heavy in the snaffle turn out to be exceptionally light with a curb bit. Therefore, if a horse was heavy in the snaffle, I don't automatically put him in a severe bit to begin with. Then I would have nowhere to go later.

As a horse develops over the years, I want to advance him into a little more sophisticated kind of bit so he'll stay light. I don't want to advance him so quickly I don't have anything left to go to. It's like

In the top picture, the horse's nose is out a little too far in an otherwise nice stop. As he finishes the stop (below), he brings his nose in, flexing more at the poll in response to the hackamore.

193

When a horse moves into the bridle, I sometimes ride with romal reins. This shows the correct position for holding them. I like to train with romal reins because you must ride with both reins even and your hand completely around them. With split reins, a rider has a tendency to slip the reins, using the direct rein to guide the nose. So it's good practice for the rider to use romal reins to check to see how well the horse is working off the neck rein, keeping his head in the correct position.

saying, "My horse is heavy in the snaffle so I'm going to put a thin, twisted-wire snaffle on him, tie his mouth shut, and rough up his mouth to get him light."

It would be better to take your time and allow this horse to find out by himself how to be light. You do this by using your hands in the proper manner, keeping them light, and after you reprimand the horse, becoming light again. This works much better than trapping a horse in a situation where, because of soreness, he becomes light temporarily, because just as surely as the sun always rises in the east, he'll get heavy again.

You have to look at training as a long-range project. If you approach it from the standpoint that "I've got to make him do this by tomorrow," he won't last very long.

I got off the track here, so let's go back to putting the horse in the hackamore and bridle. When I'm riding in the two reins, as it's called (because there are two sets of reins), I hold the bridle reins differently. Let's assume I plan to work the horse on some maneuvers to the right. I put both bridle reins in my left hand, along with the left hackamore rein, and hold the right

hackamore rein in my right hand.

As I ask the horse to circle or turn, I can use an indirect rein on the left side of his neck, and help him by giving a direct pull on the right hackamore rein.

When I plan to turn the horse to the left, I change hands, putting the bridle reins and right hackamore rein in my right hand, and left hackamore rein in my left hand.

This helps the horse learn to neckrein, and to maintain the basic correct position when I ask him to turn around. The first thing I want him to do in a turn-around is get on his hocks. Second is to start turning his head and neck. Then I want him to move his front end, stay on his inside pivot foot, and turn. By holding the reins in this manner, I can help him turn correctly without him becoming frustrated or confused, as he would if I were suddenly using just one hand instead of two.

I ride him in the two reins until I no longer have to use the hackamore reins to help him stop, turn, or do anything else. This takes a lot of time, and I don't want to dwell on it here. Just go slowly and easily. I don't ever rush a horse in the bridle. I take my time, and do everything methodically. I don't want to confuse the horse now that he's in the bridle, because I'm going to set his foundation in the bridle for the rest of his life.

Skipping the Hackamore

A lot of people go right from the snaffle to the bridle, and that's all right. I've darn sure done it myself with quite a few horses. I will only say that if you go right to the bridle, you should ride with two hands and give the horse direction. You should also do this for a much longer period of time than if you had taken him through the hackamore stage. You should always be aware of what the horse is doing with his head, because it's so easy for it to get out of position, especially if you go to neck-reining too soon.

I also want to mention that I frequently put a horse back in the snaffle for schooling. I put his foundation on him with the snaffle, and the foundation is something to build on as well as something to go back to.

When riding with romal reins, I sometimes use a fence to help the horse position his head correctly in a turn. This is especially helpful when he's first learning to respond to a neck-rein only.

16 RUNNING A PATTERN

Even if I think I know the pattern, I get the rule book and study the pattern to make sure I know it exactly.

ONE THING YOU should do before the class, or even before the show starts, is to study the pattern and the footing in the arena. Know where, or approximately where, the best ground is, especially for making your stops.

Check for dips, holes, and bad ground. Try to avoid ground that is uneven, sticky, or wet where you have to stop. Sometimes you can do this just by moving a few feet to one side in your run-downs. Study the ground before the class because you should not be looking for good ground while you are running. If you do, your body language can make your horse anticipate the stops, even though you may not be aware of it. The horse will pick up those subtle signals that might cause him to anticipate.

Stopping a reining horse is akin to riding a jumping horse; you never look at the fence immediately in front of you—you look at the next fence. On a reining horse, look beyond where you are going to stop. Look at the arena fence, or even a point beyond that when making your run-downs. This will help keep the horse from anticipating, and will also help to keep you relaxed so you don't tighten up.

Make sure you have studied the pattern thoroughly, step by step. Even if I think I know the pattern, I get the rule book and study the pattern to make sure I know it exactly. If you have never run the pattern, it's a good idea to walk through it on foot.

Also make sure your horse is thoroughly warmed up. Horses vary in how much loping they need before they are ready to be shown. Each one has a point he reaches when he begins to relax, and it's important that you know what it is.

Many horses give this indication when, while being loped, they relax and put their heads down a little bit. Or, as soon as they really give to the bridle and become relaxed and flexible, it means they are ready. Or, if they have been gawking at all the sights, they start giving you their undivided attention.

Each horse gives his own indication(s) of when he's ready. Observing how much warming up he needs at home or at schooling shows will help you learn just what it is. This is almost as important as practicing the actual maneuvers in a reining pattern.

Although the appearance of your horse and gear has no direct effect on your score, both your horse and gear should be cleaned up. A clean, well-groomed horse and neat, clean tack make a better overall impression on the judge, as does your own appearance. And after all, this is a *show*.

Something else even more important: Check your gear! If your bridle and reins have Chicago screws, make sure they are tight. Make sure the curb strap or chain is securely attached. Make sure your cinch is snug. Many a rider has self-destructed in the show ring when a piece of gear has broken or the saddle has turned.

Okay. Let's assume that the judge has asked for NRHA Pattern 6. I've gone over the pattern in my mind, step by step. I have run it mentally, knowing just where to ask my horse for his strong points, and where I'm going to ease up. If I have the opportunity, I like to watch a few horses ahead of me run the pattern. This helps set the pattern in my mind even better.

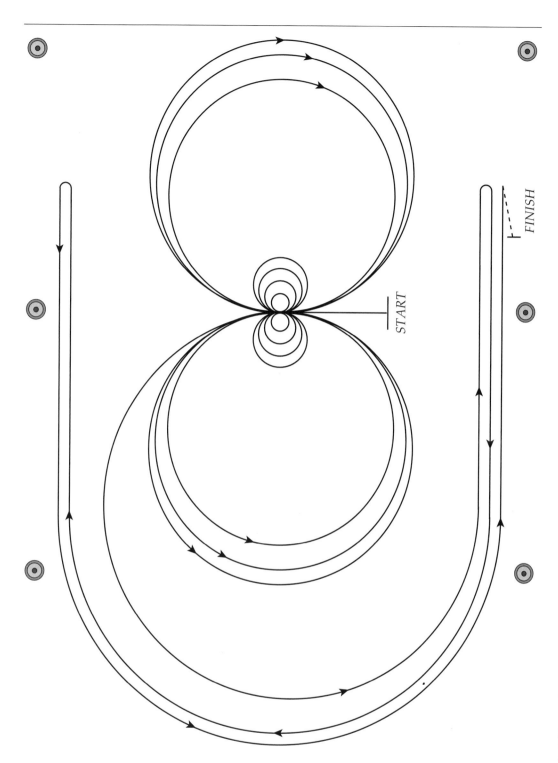

NRHA Pattern 6

Begin at the center of the arena facing the left wall.

1/ Complete four spins to the right.

2/ Complete four spins to the left. Hesitate.

3/ Beginning on the left lead, complete three circles to the left: the first two circles large and fast; the third circle small and slow. Change leads at the center of the arena.

4/ Complete three circles to the right: the first two large and fast; the third circle small and slow. Change leads at the center of the arena.

5/ Begin a large fast circle to the left but do not close this circle. Run up the right side of the arena past the center marker and do a right rollback at least 20 feet from the wall—no hesitation.

6/ Continue back around previous circle but do not close this circle. Run up the left side of the arena past the center marker and do a right rollback at least 20 feet from the wall—no hesitation.

7/ Continue back around previous circle but do not close this circle. Run up the right side of the arena past the center marker and do a sliding stop at least 20 feet from the wall or fence. Back up at least 10 feet. Hesitate to demonstrate the completion of the pattern.

Rider must drop bridle to the designated judge.

Reprinted Courtesy of National Reining Horse Association, Suite 204, 448 Main St., Coshocton, OH 43812; 614-623-0055.

First Maneuver

This pattern first calls for turn-arounds in the middle of the arena, with the first four going to the right. As I walk in, I want the horse to stay collected. I don't allow him to raise his head and look around, because I want him to have his full attention on me. I want him to be on his toes and to be thinking, so he's prepared for what I'm going to ask him. As I'm walking, I might move my hand up and down slightly to continue to remind the horse that he must be obedient to the bridle, giving at the poll and staying flexible and relaxed.

When I reach the center, I stop, make sure the horse is standing straight, and wait a few seconds while he settles. I do this because I don't want to stop and then abruptly go right into my first turn-around. I want to make sure he is ready

Once the horse has his speed and is turning well, I lower my hand to make sure I am not dragging the outside rein on his neck. When that happens, it can cause the horse to reverse his arc and drop his inside shoulder. It can also choke the motion out of him.

and aware of what I am about to ask.

Once I know I have his full attention, I start to rock my legs a little bit, as if I'm going to ask him to walk forward. Because of the way I have trained my horse, he starts to flex at the poll and put his body into a forward-motion frame. That allows me to start the turn-around without the horse taking a step or two back. That can cause problems such as backing into the turn-around or "spiraling" in his turns. This happens when he must change his

pivot foot because he was rocked back too far when he began his turns.

As I rock my legs I move my rein hand forward a little and slightly to the right, directing my horse into the right turn-around.

Some horses start a turn real fast, and some start with a few slower steps to get their foot pattern down correctly. I don't care which my horse does. If he starts slow, I cluck to him to speed him up, or use my outside foot to encourage him to go faster.

If he starts fast, I want him to stay at the same speed every turn. I would say it's almost better to start a little slower, then speed up and get into a good rhythm and hold it.

The pattern calls for four turn-arounds, and counting them as you are spinning can be a problem. It's not at all unusual for a rider to under- or over-spin. What works best for me is to count, "One, two, three, STOP." If you say "four" instead of "stop," often you'll make another turn, which will be five, and you are off pattern.

On each of my horses, I know exactly when and where I need to start shutting him down so he stops exactly where he started. If, for example, a horse turns rapidly and with a long reach in front, I say whoa about a quarter-turn from the finish. If a horse has a quick short step, I say whoa an eighth of a turn from the finish. Not stopping exactly where you started results in a penalty.

All right, I've counted "one, two, three, STOP," said whoa, and stopped as straight as I possibly can after the four spins. I release the reins very slightly and let the horse stand there and settle for a few seconds. Not allowing the horse to settle and get his bearings might cause him to go into the next set of turns incorrectly.

Now I repeat the same maneuver to the left. I rock my legs a little bit to ask the horse to rock forward, and move my rein hand forward and a little to the left, toward his left ear. When the horse rocks forward, he will usually cross over on the first step. If he gets started correctly, he will usually stay correct in all four turns. As he starts turning, I quit rocking my legs because I already have his forward motion going.

I cluck a little bit because I want the

horse to speed up. He knows what it means when I cluck or nudge him in the belly, or move my hand across his neck, applying more neck rein.

Once he has his motion going and is turning well, I lower my hand to make sure I am not dragging the outside rein on his neck as he turns. If you constantly drag your hand on the neck, it can cause him to reverse his arc, looking to the outside of the turn, and to drop his inside shoulder. It can also choke the motion out of him.

I count the same way—"One, two, three, STOP"—and after the fourth turn, stop him exactly where I started, facing the middle marker on the left wall. I let my horse settle a few seconds while making sure my saddle is straight and that I'm sitting in the middle of it.

If the horse is the kind who allows me to do it, I give him a little slack and let him stand there, relaxing his head and neck. The more I can show a horse relaxed, the longer his career will be.

On the other hand, a horse who is more hyper is more difficult to keep going, run after run after run, because he's always trying to outthink you. So it's good if you can stand and relax your horse for a few seconds in the middle of the pen.

First Set of Circles

The pattern now calls for three circles to the left, the first two large and fast, the third one slow and small, then change leads and move into the next set of circles.

To pick up the lope, I once again rock both of my legs against the horse, but this time, instead of directing him into a turn, I keep my hand centered over his neck and let him take one or two steps forward. Then, to pick up the left lead, I move my left leg away and keep my right leg against him. I also pick the horse up and hold his shoulders to the right a little to make sure his left shoulder doesn't jump to the left. I want him to lope off in a straight line. I might also cluck once or twice.

I speed the horse up so that when I enter the second quarter of the circle, I have my speed just about where I want it for the first two circles. I make sure my rein hand stays over the middle of the neck for two reasons: 1/ So the horse

When a horse turns rapidly and has a long reach, I say whoa about a quarter-turn from where I want him to stop. That shuts him down so he stops exactly where he started.

cannot drop his inside shoulder, and 2/ so I don't rein him too far to the inside. I have to stay an equal distance from both fences. If I'm 10 feet from the fence or wall in the first quarter of my circle, I have to be 10 feet from the fence on the other side of the arena. I also want to make symmetrically round circles.

After completing the first circle, some horses start anticipating a lead change or a

When I'm circling, I keep my rein hand right over the middle of the horse so I don't rein too far to the inside, which could result in the horse dropping his inside shoulder.

Photo by Rick Swan

change of speed as they come across the middle of the arena. So as I come across the middle, I continue to sit very quietly and keep the horse between my legs so he continues to travel straight, at the same rate of speed. I also keep him between the reins, but am directing him to stay in a circle to the left with a very light neck rein. I aim him toward what I call "first base" (see the Circles chapter).

I duplicate my first circle, traveling right over the top of my tracks. After I pass third base and start toward the center, I begin thinking about slowing down.

With those horses not easy to slow down, you have to start before you get to the imaginary straight line as you come across the middle. With other horses who slow immediately when you ask them, it's really cool if you can do it right in the center of the arena. Then there are those horses who slow down too fast. Before I

ask one of them to slow, I wait until I have him aimed into the smaller, slower circle. If I do it too soon, he might change leads, or even stop. Once he's aimed into the new circle, then I pick up the reins and ask him to slow.

One thing I do to slow a horse is to "quit riding fast." That is, I just relax, melt down into the saddle, and move both my legs away from the horse. Whereas I had been leaning forward slightly in my fast circles, I now sit up straight. This signals the horse to pick up a slower cadence.

With some horses, that's all that's necessary to slow them. But with most horses, you slow them by picking up the reins a little bit and asking them to bridle up (flex at the poll). A lot of horses look as if they have slowed, before they actually have, when their heads go from slightly in front of the vertical with their noses out, to a vertical position. So you can sometimes create a slower impression by just sitting straight and picking up your hand so the horse's head becomes vertical. Then as you go into your smaller circle, that will automatically slow the horse somewhat.

In the small, slow circle, I keep a good, rhythmic three-beat lope. Therefore I don't want to make such a small circle, or go into it so sharply, that the horse's movement becomes choppy. I don't want to slow so much, either, that the horse might drop to a trot. That will result in a penalty for breaking gait.

Changing Leads

As I come across the middle again, this time I have to change leads. So as I approach the center, I pick the reins up to get my horse's body straight. At the same time I add a little pressure from my right leg. Why? Since the horse has been traveling in a left circle, his body has been in a left arc, with his rib cage slightly to the right. I want his body absolutely straight to change leads, so I apply some pressure from my right leg to move his rib cage to the left, making his body straight as an arrow as we come across the middle.

As I reach the center, I pick the reins up slightly and keep my rein hand a little to the left to keep the shoulders to the left.

Now I maybe cluck once or twice, release my right leg, and the horse will change to the right lead.

When I pick up the reins to hold the shoulders over, I sometimes cluck in order to maintain the horse's cadence—to prevent him from slowing down. Whether I cluck depends on the individual horse; if one is not apt to slow down, I don't cluck. Eventually a cluck, along with other signals, can become a cue to change leads.

After the horse changes, I keep him going straight for a couple of strides, then head into my first right circle.

Second Set of Circles

Because I want to run a balanced pattern, I want these circles to be exactly the same size and speed as my left set of circles. So as I speed up going into the first quarter of the circle and aim toward first base, I decide how far away from the fence I should be. It should be the same distance as in my first set of circles. I gallop the second large, fast circle right on top of the tracks of my first circle.

As I complete the second circle, I know my horse well enough to realize exactly when I need to ask him to start slowing for the small circle as I come across the middle. If my small, slow circle to the left was half as big as my large, fast circles, I want my small, slow to the right to be exactly half the size of the larger ones. I also want my speed to be exactly the same. That's very important. Equally important is coming across the exact center of the arena each time. Judges can "plus" or "minus" your score, depending on how well you do these things.

Changing Leads Again

As I finish the small, slow circle and approach the middle, I straighten the horse by reining him slightly to the right and by putting my left leg on him to move his rib cage to the right. I get him dead straight, hold him that way for a stride or two, and then on a down stride I maybe cluck once or twice, release my left leg, and he will change leads.

I hold him straight for a couple of

In a run-down, I let the horse gradually build to his optimum speed, the best speed from which he stops. Then I maintain that speed until I'm ready to stop.

strides, then release the reins slightly and aim him into the first quarter of a large, fast circle to the left. But this time I do not close the circle. The rule book reads: "Begin a large, fast circle to the left but do not close this circle." Instead you run up the right side of the arena past the center marker, and do a right rollback at least 20 feet from the wall or fence, with no hesitation.

After I change leads, I start the circle at exactly the same speed and size as my large, fast circles that I did earlier.

First Run-Down and Stop

As I straighten out and head toward my first stop, I have to make decisions very quickly.

First, do I want to take a little more

I allow the horse to begin his stop without my pulling on the reins because I want him to start sliding. A split second after I say whoa, the horse melts into the ground (top). As he continues to slide, I have raised my rein hand slightly to balance him.

hold of my horse so I have a bit more control? This depends on the horse, whether he can be galloping freely as he makes his approach to the stop, or if he needs more contact so he's thinking a little bit more about me. Second, where am I going to stop? Even though I checked the ground before the class started, it might have changed, especially where everyone else has been stopping. That ground might be all chopped up by now, so I don't want to stop there.

The pattern requires that run-downs and stops be at least 20 feet away from the fence. But, I can move farther away if there's better ground, say 30 feet away from the fence. Arenas that are exceptionally wide, such as 150 feet, allow you to do this and still leave sufficient distance between your run-downs on each side of the arena.

Lengthwise, you must go beyond the center marker before stopping. Again, depending on the ground, you might want to go significantly farther, but not so far it looks like you are fencing your horse.

I always like to go some distance beyond the center marker. I don't want my horse to think that as soon as he reaches top speed and passes the center marker that I'm going to shut him off right there.

Some riders have a tendency to wait, gaining speed late in the run-down, and as soon as the horse is going fast, they immediately ask the horse to stop. Well, after a horse has been shown several times like that, as soon as he reaches optimum speed, he starts thinking *stop*. Sometimes he won't even reach optimum speed before he begins anticipating the stop.

I consider optimum speed as the best speed my horse stops from. Some horses can run wide open and stop beautifully; others might need to be geared down to a fast gallop.

So as I come around the corner and go into the run-down, I rate my horse until he reaches his optimum speed. When he reaches that speed, I let him continue to stride at that pace. It's like swinging a rope. Just as you would swing, swing, swing your loop, the horse strides, strides, and strides at the speed from which he stops best.

I want to emphasize *straight*, because

it's so important that the horse runs straight. If he's veering a bit from one side to the other, or dropping one shoulder or the other, he cannot stop his best.

Okay. I'm well past the center marker, the horse is running at optimum speed, and I've reached the point where I want to stop. I give my horse a little slack in the reins, sit down in the saddle, and say whoa. I allow him to begin the stop without my pulling on the reins because I want him to start sliding. Actually, as soon as I say whoa, the horse will reach out with his nose, taking the slack out of my reins. Then, I just try to balance the horse on the bridle and allow him to slide.

Whether I have to pull on the reins depends on the ground and the horse. If it's heavy ground, I might have to help him with a light pull. Some horses always need a light pull, regardless of the ground conditions. But I try never to pull hard. The harder you pull, the shorter the slide, usually.

First Rollback

When I feel his motion has completely stopped at the end of his slide, I ask him to roll back without hesitating. I raise my rein hand, almost as if I were going to ask him to back, but I move my hand slightly to the right because we have to roll back to the right, over the same tracks we made coming into the stop.

As I move my rein hand to the right, the horse rocks back slightly on his hocks and then starts to come around in response to the neck-rein. When he's about halfway through the turn, I start releasing the neck-rein pressure and add pressure from my left leg. That cues the horse to get his left ribs under him and to pick up the right lead as we come out of the rollback. I want to be on the correct lead as he comes out of the rollback and as we go around the top of the arena.

It's important that the horse gallops out of the rollback because trotting out results in a penalty. So as the horse is finishing rolling back, I might cluck to him for impulsion. Depending on the horse, I might rise out of the saddle somewhat or sit back to drive him forward, whichever works best for that horse.

While he has been rolling back, I keep my hand quiet so he stays in the bridle, not throwing his head.

Second Run-Down and Stop

Now we gallop toward the top of the arena, around the corner, and down the other side. With some horses, you can gallop toward the top of the circle a little faster. With other horses, you might need a little more contact on the bridle so they stay under full control.

I usually rate my horse's speed because I don't want him running wide open as we go around the corner. I want a lot of control so that he runs straight, and stays straight between my reins and my legs.

The more control you can keep on a horse, the better he will perform and the longer his show career will last. Why? Control helps prevent him from anticipating. If he continually anticipates, the problem will become worse, and then he will need more schooling. Any horse who needs an extreme amount of schooling simply will not last very long. It's too demanding on his body and mind.

As I come around the top of the pen, again I have to think about where the best stopping area is. I also pay strict attention to keeping the horse galloping straight, parallel to the fence, and at least 20 feet away from it.

I gradually let my horse go faster until he has reached the optimum speed from which he stops best. Then when I'm well past the marker, so I don't have any doubt about stopping too soon, I move my rein hand slightly forward, sit down, say whoa, and let him slide.

Second Rollback

When I feel the horse's motion has completely stopped, I ask him to roll back to the left. This time as I pick up my rein

The more control you can keep on a horse, the better he will perform and the longer his show career will last.

203

*It's extremely important
that a horse runs straight.
If he's veering or leaning
to one side, or dropping
a shoulder, he cannot
stop well. This sequence
of three photos depicts
Seven S Catalpa running
straight and true (1).
When I ask her to stop (2),
I give her a little slack, sit
down, and say whoa.
After she stops (3), I hesitate a few seconds, letting
her gather herself before I
ask her for the next
maneuver.*

Photos by Rick Swan

1/

2/

hand (my left) and move it to the left, I am
careful not to drag my hand too low or too
far. When I roll back to the right, I don't
have to worry about that because I have to
bring my rein hand across my body.
Therefore, I'm not as apt to move my hand
too far to the right. But it could happen in
a left rollback if I'm not careful.

Dragging your rein hand too far either
way can pull the horse out of the ground, so
his hindquarters swing out and his front end
turns too far. Then he will usually pick up
the incorrect lead as he breaks into a gallop.

To reiterate, I initiate the rollback with
a light neck-rein. Then about halfway
through the turn, I release the neck-rein,
apply pressure from my right leg, and
cluck. If everything goes smoothly and
correctly, my horse breaks into a gallop on
the left lead, covering the same tracks we
made coming into the stop.

Third Run-Down, Stop, Back

Again, I rate my horse's speed as we
come around the top of the pen. As we
straighten out, I look ahead and aim the

3/

204

horse for some fresh ground, if possible. I let him reach his optimum stopping speed and hold it . . . hold it . . . hold it, being very careful that he is running straight. I can't emphasize that enough!

Since we rolled back to the right the previous time we came down this side of the arena, the horse may be thinking *rollback* again. While we are galloping down the arena, he might start veering or drifting to the right. If this happens, I use my reins and right leg to straighten him up. Sometimes a young horse will be a little leery of the fence or the wall and may drift toward the center. In that case, I use my reins and inside leg to straighten him up.

Once again, when I am well past the center marker, I give the horse a little slack, sit down, and say whoa. Since we just made two stops followed immediately by rollbacks, the horse might still be thinking *rollback*. Therefore I'm very careful to keep him right between the reins and my legs as he finishes his stop, so he can't start to turn.

I let him hesitate just a second or two after he finishes the stop, then ask him to back. Here again, a shifty or quick-footed horse might still be thinking rollback, and if he starts to turn, you will be penalized, or even DQed if he goes too far. So I keep the horse right between my legs and reins.

To initiate the back-up, I take a light pull on the reins, just enough to get his motion started and to make him bridle up and flex at the poll. To ask for more speed, I use my legs on some horses; with others, I just cluck. One thing I don't do is pull hard! That raises the head and makes the back concave, which doesn't allow the horse to get his back legs under him. Which, in turn, makes it physically impossible for him to back faster.

When I use my legs to ask for more speed, I just rock them back and forth against the horse's sides. I can also use my legs to straighten the horse if he starts to back crooked. This should not happen, however, if he has been trained correctly, and if I have my reins even, and am not pressuring him with one leg more than the other.

The rules require at least a 10-foot back-up. To be safe, I usually back between 12 and 15 feet . . . straight, true, and fast. Then the rules state that you must hesitate to indicate the completion of the pattern.

So I release my rein pressure, say whoa, and maybe pat or stroke the horse on the neck to help him relax.

Then I ride to the designated judge for the bridle check. Sometimes this judge is at the gate, outside of the arena. If he (or she) is inside the arena, ride over, dismount, and drop your bridle. Then lead your horse out of the arena quickly so you get out of the way of the next horse. That's a courtesy to the judge.

Review

I think it's important that you review each run you make and learn what you need to correct before your next pattern. Maybe your horse was dropping his inside shoulder in his left set of circles. Or maybe he was pushy in the run-down, pulling on the bridle too much. Or maybe when you sat down and said whoa, he didn't go into the stop as quickly as you wanted him to. Maybe it was because your timing was off. Watching a videotape of your run can be very enlightening, and well worth the cost if you have to pay the show's video photographer.

When I show, the main thing I don't want to do is over-ride my horse. I want him to do what he can do best. If I see someone else in my class turning around faster than my horse can, I won't try to speed my horse up because then his form might not be correct. If he presently can only turn around at medium speed, but with good rhythm, that's what I'll ask him to do at the show. I will improve his speed at home, while schooling.

In summary, ride your horse to his best advantage. Take advantage of his strong points, and try to cover up his weak points. Also remember that when your horse has correct form, and when you ride a precise, correct pattern, your chances of winning are probably greater than someone who rides a faster, flashier horse, but whose form and pattern tend to be sloppy.

Ride your horse to his best advantage.

17 PSYCHOLOGY OF TRAINING

You should tailor your training program to fit each horse.

AS HORSEMEN KNOW, every horse is an individual. Each one has his own personality, temperament, quirks, likes and dislikes, sensitivity (or lack of), and level of intelligence.

Never is this knowledge of how horses differ more important than in training, because what works on ol' Bay might backfire on ol' Sorrely. This doesn't mean that you get away from your basic fundamentals, but that you tailor your training program to fit each horse. It's like looking at a road map that shows several possible routes to your destination; you pick the one that best suits you. In training, you pick the route that best fits each horse.

Because horses are individuals, they vary in how much work they need. Some need to be ridden 5 or 6 days a week; others get along better on fewer days, and just about every horse benefits from an occasional vacation.

I ride my horses an average of 4 days a week, and when I'm out of town, they are generally turned out every day for free exercise, or ridden by one of my assistants to keep them legged up. They don't get any schooling, just riding. Often when I return and get back on a particular horse, I'm surprised at how well he is doing—he may be better than he ever was.

Sometimes he actually *is* better. After having a vacation, he has had time to absorb his training. But sometimes it's just that I can see him in a better perspective. It's like watching a youngster grow. When you see him every day, he doesn't seem to be growing at all. But when you return home after being away for a week, it seems as if he's shot up 3 inches.

Although I ride my horses 4 days a week, I'm not training on them all the time, especially a reining horse. You have to let a reining horse relax and gather his thoughts. That's when I ride him outside of the arena. I loosen up the reins, let him drop his head, and do a lot of quiet walking, jogging, and loping.

I can't emphasize enough how important this is . . . getting the horse away from the barn and arena and letting him relax and look around. It keeps him fresh, and really helps to prevent problems from developing—problems like tail switching,

After a horse has performed a maneuver well, I like to let him stand a minute or two as a reward, and to take the pressure off him. This horse has just completed a sliding stop.

anticipating lead changes, scotching on run-downs, and a generally unhappy appearance and attitude. Drilling a horse continually on any event or maneuver will soon destroy his enthusiasm for it, and lead to bad habits.

Even when I am working a horse in the arena, I do not work him on all parts of the reining pattern every time I ride him. One day, for example, I might work him on stops. I'll gallop around the arena, or diagonally across it, and stop at various places. He never knows when or where I might ask him to stop, or if I will ask him to keep running.

On the next day, maybe I'll lope circles, working on correct positioning. The third day, I might work on turn-arounds. On the fourth day, I might work on overall flexibility. Or I might let him follow some cows around in the cutting pen—just to do something different with him to keep his mind fresh, even though he may never make a working cow horse or cutting horse.

To help keep the mind of a reining horse fresh, I will let him follow some cows around in the cutting pen.

A horse doesn't need to be ridden every day to progress.

Some days, I might ride him outside the arena, on a loose rein, and let him totally relax while we jog and lope. On his days off, he is turned out for further relaxation. A horse doesn't need to be ridden every day to progress. In fact, some horses improve faster when ridden only every other day.

One thing I rarely do at home is work a horse on patterns. I school him on various parts of the pattern, as I've already mentioned, and once he knows all of them, it's easy to put them together in the show ring. This helps prevent the horse from anticipating what's next when actually running a pattern.

However, I sometimes have my non-pro riders run patterns so I can critique them. This helps them to run better patterns at shows. In these situations, I'm working on the rider, not the horse.

Occasionally I'm asked how I would start an older horse on reining, such as a horse who's only been been ridden for pleasure. A lot depends on his age, how set he is in his ways, and how well he has been trained. I want to emphasize that it is much easier to teach a 2-year-old than it is an older horse who has perhaps developed bad habits and defense mechanisms.

But generally, I'd start an older horse as if he were a colt. I'd put him in a snaffle bit, see if he understands leg pressure, make sure he's got a good back-up and a 180-degree turn, and make sure his mouth is right before going on to fancy things.

Just because he's broke doesn't mean you can knock on him to turn around, or pull on him to get him to stop. You've got to go back to the basics and make him understand these new things. However, he can probably advance much faster than a colt if he's already been in the bridle, is well-broke, and—most important—has no serious problems.

When you are training, there is no place for anger. Every good trainer knows that, and it's easy to say it, but usually we all have to learn the hard way how true it is.

I like to turn my horses loose in the arena frequently, so they can run and play. I also have two grass paddocks in which we turn our show horses loose for a few hours several days a week. That gets them out of their stalls, allows them some green grass, and gives them a relaxing break from training.

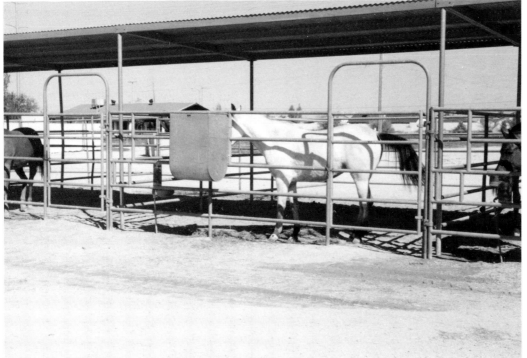

In addition to my show barn I also have outside pens where we keep some horses. We often put some of the stalled horses in outside pens for a few hours a day just to get them out of their stalls, and so they can see what's going on around the ranch.

The opportunity for a colt or any horse to move cattle can do wonders for their training and mental attitude. This young palomino had never seen cattle before, and they have his full attention. The rider is Rick Swan, Western Horseman's advertising assistant.

Obviously if a horse reaches around and bites your foot, that's darn sure a time to reprimand him. But discipline him in a manner he understands, then quit. Don't keep on. That will only make him fear you instead of respect you, and might also make him rebellious.

When you get on a horse, don't have vengeance in your heart. If you are upset because your wife's mad at you, or the last horse you rode was difficult, let those emotions go. If you take your anger out on the next horse you ride, you might set his training back several weeks.

Don't forget that horses have feelings, too. If they could talk, I believe they'd tell us a few things about themselves that would help us in training them. We have to realize that they have good days and bad days, just like we do, and that they probably have some of the same ailments we do, especially stiffness, sore muscles, and aching joints. They can't tell us about them, except through obvious lameness.

If a horse is suddenly having difficulty performing a maneuver that you know he can do very well, don't automatically assume he's being stubborn. Find out if he's hurting.

That's why a rider must be sensitive to how his horse feels, and realize when a horse is having a bad day, he can't possibly give his maximum. We cannot expect 100 percent every time we ride our horses.

Suppose a horse isn't doing something quite right, like turning around. You school him and feel that you've done your best to get the point across to him, but he's still not right. Rather than get in a storm with him, it would be better to put him up and let him rest. When you get on him the next day, he might do it just fine. Maybe he absorbed the lesson during the night, or maybe if he had been a little stiff or sore, he's okay now.

Sometimes when I'm having a problem with a horse, I get off in the arena, dally the reins around the horn, and let him wander around loose while I ride another horse. I think about the problem, what's causing it, and what I should be doing to correct it. When I get back on the horse, he's not hot, he's not mad, and I can begin to work out the sequence of correction. If I'd gone ahead with the horse and gotten in a storm with him, the only thing that would come out of it would be an intimidated or confused horse.

By staying calm and cool, and keeping your wits about you, you can achieve optimum results from your correction. You can't if you get mad and go to thrashing. You must also realize exactly what to do to correct a horse to achieve the result you want.

There are many analogies between humans and horses, and training a young horse is just like training a child. You reprimand them when they are wrong, and praise them when they are right. And praise should be more than just absence of punishment.

To praise a horse, I like to drop the reins, let him stand, and stroke him on the neck. To correct him, I can use my hands, legs, or the ends of the reins, whichever is appropriate.

There are also indirect ways you can reward a horse, like taking good care of him, which, of course, should be standard procedure. Providing him a comfortable place to stay, feeding him properly, keeping him well-groomed, and turning him out so he can run and play . . . those things not only keep him feeling good, but are a reward too. They make him feel wanted and appreciated, and he'll respond to that just like a person would.

Note: The bits and other equipment shown in this book can be purchased at many tack stores, or from AD Tack in Scottsdale, Arizona. This is a mail-order firm only, not a store. Ph. 602-451-3305; FAX 602-391-1469.

18 PSYCHOLOGY OF SHOWING

Always show your horse in the style or fashion that fits him best.

BEFORE I EVER SHOW a young horse, I like to trailer him to other arenas as well as to horse shows, where I just ride him around the grounds. This gets him accustomed to being trailered and lets him get acquainted and relaxed with different sights and sounds. My goal is not to train or put any pressure on him.

This experience plays a big role in getting a horse ready to show. At most reining futurities you can usually spot horses who have never been off the ranch. They get spooked if it's a big indoor arena or coliseum, they gawk at the audience, and

are rattled by applause. The presence of photographers and judges standing or seated in the arena can also distract them. Their attention is everywhere but on the rider, which makes it very difficult to get them shown to the best of their ability.

If they are not used to being hauled, drinking strange water, and being in an unfamiliar barn, they will not be in the best shape to show. Sometimes lights and activity in the barn all night long will not allow them to rest properly. But, they have to get accustomed to it.

Taking a horse to a new place will also

Sometimes the presence of judges, scribes, and photographers in the arena distracts the attention of a young horse being shown the first few times.

Photo by Fran Smith

tell me how he's going to act in an atmosphere that differs from his home environment. Does he get nervous and uptight? Or does he stay calm and take everything in stride? A horse who gets hyper may take more riding before his class to help him settle, whereas others need to be ridden just enough to loosen their muscles.

A lot of riders beat themselves in a reining class by overschooling before the class. This is called "leaving the work in the practice pen," and it will take the brilliance off your work. In warming the horse up, use wise judgment and loosen him up just enough to prepare him to show to the peak of his ability.

Always remember the fundamentals: the position you want the horse to be in when you turn him around, and how you want him to stop. Don't get excited and forget how you do things, like sitting down and saying whoa before taking hold of his head when asking him to stop.

In actually running a pattern, stay calm. Don't let your adrenalin pump you up so much that you put more pressure on the horse than he can handle—to the point that he doesn't even perform as well as he can at home. Show the horse only to his capability; do not push him to try to beat a horse who perhaps has more talent or experience. In doing that, you might blow your whole run and not even place. You might create problems in the horse that will hinder him later on when he is ready for a pressure run.

It is important to remember that win, lose, or draw, there will always be another horse show, and there will always be another horse. Try to make this horse work the best that he possibly can at his present stage of training, and be satisfied that you have done that kind of job.

Although I like to win as much as anybody, I am more interested in showing off my horse's ability and my workmanship—how I've trained and prepared the horse—than I am in the placings. That's why I never try to beat somebody else. I simply show my horse to his maximum capability. I don't go into a class with the thought, *I am going to win,* and pressure my horse beyond his ability or readiness. But if he has been prepared, seasoned, and has the talent, I darn sure ride him to his maximum capability.

When watching a reining run, the judge is looking at the overall picture, so know how your horse looks the prettiest and smoothest. In my opinion, position and control are far more important than speed. It's better to travel at a moderate speed and have good form than it is to highball through the pattern with rough circles, bad stops, and U-turn rollbacks. If a horse can handle a lot of speed and still maintain form, great. But if not, throttle him down a few notches and keep his form correct. Also remember his strong points and try to capitalize on them, and smooth over his weaker points the best you can.

If he's a good, hard stopper, razzle-dazzle the judge and crowds with your stops. If he's not flashy in his turn-arounds, turn easy and try to keep his form correct.

You have to be thinking all the time, not only how to best show the horse, but also to stay on pattern. That's not always easy, and even the best of riders occasionally go off pattern. If it happens to you, don't let it eat at you; there's always another show.

A lot of success in showing depends on your not getting nervous, and keeping your wits about you. Don't let the runs that precede you bother you. Sometimes it's better not to watch them. Don't let the performances of other horses in the warm-up pen dictate how you're going to show your horse. Always show your horse in the style or fashion that fits him best. Don't try to show him according to the way others are showing their horses.

Maybe some of the other horses can handle more speed or turn around faster than your horse. But maybe your horse can run a more precise pattern, with prettier circles and changes.

I guarantee that if you keep your cool and make a nice, correct run, your turn to win will come over a rider who runs hard, but makes a lot of mistakes. He might score higher than you today, but if you concentrate on building a foundation and correct positioning on your horse, you'll end up winning when your horse is ready. In the long run, your horse will benefit from your patience

I don't mean to imply, however, that you should always run an easy-going pattern. When your horse is ready, show him to win!

IN THIS ERA of specialists in the horse show world, Al Dunning stands out as one who has, and still can, train horses successfully for a number of events. In years past, he owned or campaigned top halter horses, such as Ricky Bonanza, the 1970 AQHA Honor Roll halter stallion, and several western pleasure and hunter-under-saddle champions.

He has won AQHA world championships in western riding, cutting, reining, and working cow horse. At the All American Quarter Horse Congress one year, he won both go-rounds and the finals of the NRHA open reining.

In the world of cutting, he has won the Tropicana Cutting Futurity, the Pacific Coast Cutting Horse Association Derby, and the Las Vegas Classic/Challenge. As a teen-ager growing up in Arizona, Al even roped and barrel raced. "We did all the things kids love to do with their horses."

But through the years, reining has remained the event he likes best, and for which he is best known. Nonetheless, Al's broad background has given him invaluable experience and knowledge, which he is generous in sharing with others. Known as a trainer's trainer, Al has helped many of his students and apprentices establish successful careers of their own. Trainers such as Pete Kyle, Casey Hinton, and Brett Stone. It's not at all unusual, either, for trainers to call Al to discuss problems they are having, or to bring horses and ride with Al for a few days.

Al gets 5 stars as a teacher of non-pros. He has the unique ability to instantly identify what a rider is doing wrong, and tell the rider exactly how to correct the problem(s). Consequently Al is in demand as a teacher and clinician. Some of his non-pro riders have won a number of major events and championships. During a 3-year period at the Quarter Horse Congress, his students won classes in horsemanship, western riding, trail, hunt-seat equitation, and hunter-under-saddle— plus two all-around youth championships.

Al's willingness to share both his time and advice is a reflection of the help he has received over the years. He also firmly believes that "we are put on this earth for a reason, and it is to share with others the knowledge the Lord has given us."

Al doesn't hesitate to give credit for his success and attitude to his strong belief in the virtues of Christianity. He is not one who pushes his religious convictions on others, but when asked, he talks about them freely. "I've come to believe that the Christian life has helped me more than anything else in becoming successful."

Al also gives generously of his time to organizations. He is presently an AQHA director and the chairman of the AQHA show & contest committee. He has served as an NCHA director and been president of the Arizona Quarter Horse Breeders Association, as well as being on their board since 1975. He was a founding member and charter president of the Arizona Quarter Horse Youth Association, and was on the stock seat committee of the American Horse Shows Association for 5 years. In the Arizona Cutting Horse Association, he has twice been president.

Al has also judged many major shows, including the AQHA World Championship Show three times, and given clinics all over the United States and in Canada, Argentina, Germany, and Australia.

The Dunning family (from left): Grady, Becky, McKenzie, and Al. The canine family members include (from left): Harley, Murphy, and Dooner. Not shown are Rascal the cat and Bella, another yellow Lab.

Although Al has not shown extensively in reining the past few years, he has certainly stayed in tune with the times. He has trained many top reining horses and coached several of the nation's best non-pro reining exhibitors.

In 1993, Al became a co-owner of Boomernic, who won the 1992 NRHA Futurity with Brett Stone as his rider. Since Al will be training several Boomernic foals every year, this has rekindled his interest in showing reiners.

Al was born in the Chicago area in 1950 and lived in Wilmette, Ill., until he was 9 years old. He learned to ride in a flat saddle on the bridle trails of Chicago-area parks. Then his family moved to Scottsdale in 1959, where Al and his sisters quickly became involved with horses. "Between the time I was 12 and 19, we owned 27 horses."

When he was 14, Al met Jim Paul, a trainer and horseman who became a major influence in Al's life. "I had never been around anyone quite like him, and to best describe him, I'd say he was darn sure what a young man would consider the John Wayne-type. He became a father image to me."

Jim also refined Al's riding skills. Consequently, Al won a truckload of year-end high-point awards in the Arizona Quarter Horse Breeders Association in the years between 1962 and 1969.

Today, Jim Paul is best known as the father of Randy and Jimmy Paul, both successful reining and cow horse trainers in the Scottsdale area. As Al says, "They were just little kids when I rode with Jim. Now I have to go out and try to beat 'em!"

In 1969 when John Hoyt was living in Scottsdale (he now lives in Texas), Al began riding with him. From John, Al learned "that you've got to have a training program you like, and one you can stick with in order for your training to have continuity and a sense of direction."

In 1970, Al quit college when he decided to become a professional trainer. Success came quickly with a number of horses, but it was a buckskin gelding named Expensive Hobby who established Al as a rising star in the reining and cow horse world. Al, however, is quick to give full credit to "Hobby," as he always referred to him. "He was a wonderful horse, with tremendous athletic ability and a great mind. He was easy to train and show, and I was honored to have him."

Hobby was owned by Georganna Stewart, who also showed the buckskin. Between Al and Georganna, Hobby won numerous championships or reserves in reining, stock horse, and cow horse events, including the Cow Palace in San Francisco, Del Mar in southern California (five championships in 5 years), and the Santa Barbara National Show. That was in the heyday of the big, open competitions on the West Coast. Al and Hobby also won the open bridle reserve championship one year at the Snaffle Bit Futurity in Reno. Hobby won over 100 firsts in reining and cow horse events.

Foaled in 1970, Hobby was retired in 1982 and lives today on Al's place where he enjoys a grassy paddock and lots of TLC. On the back cover of this book is a photograph taken in 1994 of Al with Hobby, who was 24 at the time.

In 1971 Al married the former Becky Lasley. They met in the mid-1960s through horse activities and often competed against each other in the show ring. Becky continued showing for a number of years after she and Al were married. But now she observes horse shows and cuttings from the announcer's stand. She has become a very popular announcer, and this work keeps her busy throughout the year in several western states.

Al and Becky have two children, McKenzie, born in 1979, and Grady, born in 1983. Although McKenzie is more laidback about horses than her folks are, she has successfully competed in youth cuttings.

As for Grady, he's crazy about basketball, and has already achieved all-star status as a player at basketball camps and in YMCA and Boys' Club league play.

Shortly after they were married, Al and Becky bought 10 acres of raw land northeast of Scottsdale, built their Almosta Ranch, and over the years bought several adjoining parcels for a total of 22 acres. Initially, they were surrounded by thousands of acres of desert. Now, however, the Dunnings are surrounded by thousands of town homes, condos, and private residences. Consequently, Al and Becky have purchased land northeast of the city, in an area called Rio Verde where they plan to build a brand-new version of their Almosta Ranch.—*Pat Close*

Western Horseman Magazine
Colorado Springs, Colorado

The Western Horseman, established in 1936, is the world's leading horse publication. For subscription information and to order other Western Horseman books, contact: Western Horseman, Box 7980, Colorado Springs, CO 80933-7980; 719-633-5524.

Books Published by Western Horseman Inc.

TEAM ROPING by Leo Camarillo
144 pages and 200 photographs covering every aspect of heading and heeling.

REINING, Completely Revised by Al Dunning
216 pages and over 300 photographs showing how to train horses for this popular event.

CALF ROPING by Roy Cooper
144 pages and 280 photographs covering the how-to of roping and tying.

BARREL RACING by Sharon Camarillo
144 pages and 200 photographs. Tells how to train and compete successfully.

HORSEMAN'S SCRAPBOOK by Randy Steffen
144 pages and 250 illustrations. A collection of popular handy hints.

WESTERN HORSEMANSHIP by Richard Shrake
144 pages and 150 photographs. Complete guide to riding western horses.

HEALTH PROBLEMS by Robert M. Miller, D.V.M.
144 pages on management, illness and injuries, lameness, mares and foals, and more.

CUTTING by Leon Harrel
144 pages and 200 photographs. Complete how-to guide on this popular sport.

WESTERN TRAINING by Jack Brainard
With Peter Phinny. 136 pages. Stresses the foundation for western training.

BACON & BEANS by Stella Hughes
136 pages and 200-plus recipes for popular western chow.

STARTING COLTS by Mike Kevil
168 pages and 400 photographs. Step-by-step process in starting colts.

IMPRINT TRAINING by Robert M. Miller, D.V.M.
144 pages and 250 photographs. Learn how to "program" newborn foals.

TEAM PENNING by Phil Livingston
144 pages and 200 photographs. Tells how to compete in this popular family sport.

NATURAL HORSE-MAN-SHIP by Pat Parelli
224 pages and 275 photographs. Parelli's six keys to a natural horse-human relationship.

LEGENDS by Diane C. Simmons
168 pages and 214 photographs. Includes these outstanding early-day Quarter Horse stallions and mares: Barbra B, Bert, Chicaro Bill, Cowboy P-12, Depth Charge (TB), Doc Bar, Go Man Go, Hard Twist, Hollywood Gold, Joe Hancock, Joe Reed P-3, Joe Reed II, King P-234, King Fritz, Leo, Peppy, Plaudit, Poco Bueno, Poco Tivio, Queenie, Quick M Silver, Shue Fly, Star Duster, Three Bars (TB), Top Deck (TB), and Wimpy P-1.

LEGENDS 2 by Jim Goodhue, Frank Holmes, Phil Livingston, Diane C. Simmons
192 pages and 224 photographs. Includes these outstanding Quarter Horses: Clabber, Driftwood, Easy Jet, Grey Badger II, Jessie James, Jet Deck, Joe Bailey P-4 (Gonzales), Joe Bailey (Weatherford), King's Pistol, Lena's Bar, Lightning Bar, Lucky Blanton, Midnight, Midnight Jr, Moon Deck, My Texas Dandy, Oklahoma Star, Oklahoma Star Jr., Peter McCue, Rocket Bar (TB), Skipper W, Sugar Bars, and Traveler.

ROOFS AND RAILS by Gavin Ehringer
144 pages, 128 black-and-white photographs plus drawings, charts, and floor plans. How to plan and build your ideal horse facility.

FIRST HORSE by Fran Devereux Smith
176 pages, 160 black-and-white photos, about 40 illustrations. Step-by-step, how-to information for the first-time horse owner and/or novice rider.

THE HANK WIESCAMP STORY by Frank Holmes
208 pages and over 260 photographs. The biography of the legendary breeder of Quarter Horses, Appaloosas, and Paints.